Socialism And Religion

Sixpence Nett.

Also in Quarter Cloth, gilt top, 1s. nett,

Socialism and Religion by the Revs. Stewart Headlam, Percy Dearmer & Dr. John Clifford, also by John Woolman, of the Society of Friends.

The
Fabian
Socialist
Series No. 1.

A. C.
Fifield,
44 Fleet
Street, E.C.

FABIAN SOCIALIST SERIES, No 1

Reprinted from Fabian Tracts, Revised

SOCIALISM AND RELIGION

THE FABIAN SOCIETY

FOUNDED 1883

THE FABIAN SOCIETY consists of men and women who are Socialists, that is to say, in the words of its "Basis," of those who aim at the reorganization of society by the emancipation of Land and Industrial Capital from individual and class ownership, and the vesting of them in the community for the general benefit. . . . For the attainment of these ends the Fabian Society looks to the spread of Socialist opinions, and the social and political changes consequent thereon. It seeks to promote these by the general dissemination of knowledge as to the relation between the individual and society in its economic, ethical, and political aspects.

The Society welcomes as members any persons, men or women, who desire to promote the growth of Socialist opinion and to hasten the enactment of Socialist measures, and it exacts from its members no pledge except a declaration that they are Socialists.

The Society is largely occupied in the endeavour to discover in what way the principles of Socialism can be applied both to the political problems which from time to time come up for settlement, and to those problems of the future which are as yet rather political theory than actual politics. It holds fortnightly meetings for the discussion of papers on such subjects by members and others, some of which are published as Fabian Tracts.

The Society includes :—

I. MEMBERS, who must sign the Basis and be elected by the Committee. Their subscription is no' fixed ; each is expected to pay according to his means. They control the Society through their Executive Committee and at business meetings.

II. ASSOCIATES, who sign a form expressing general sympathy with the objects of the Society, and pay not less than 10s. a year. They can attend all except specially private meetings, but have no control over the Society and its policy.

III. SUBSCRIBERS, who must pay at least 5s. a year, and can attend the lectures.

The monthly paper, "FABIAN NEWS," and the Fabian Tracts are sent as published to all three classes.

Lists of Publications, Annual Report, Form of Application as Member or Associate, and any other information can be obtained on application, personally, or by letter, of

THE SECRETARY OF THE FABIAN SOCIETY,

3 CLEMENT'S INN, STRAND, LONDON, W.C.

SOCIALISM AND RELIGION

By

THE REV. STEWART D. HEADLAM
THE REV. PERCY DEARMER
THE REV. JOHN CLIFFORD
& JOHN WOOLMAN (*of the Society of Friends*)

Fabian Socialist Series, No. 1

LONDON
A. C. FIFIELD, 44 FLEET STREET, E.C.
1908

CONTENTS

SOCIALISM
AND RELIGION

I. CHRISTIAN SOCIALISM

By the Rev. STEWART D. HEADLAM

LONG before the Fabian Society was founded I learnt the principles and was familiar with the title of "*Christian Socialism*" from Maurice and Kingsley, the Professors of Philosophy and History at Cambridge.

Heaven on earth.—There were those then, as there are those now, who object both to the title and to the principles it expresses : the connection of the adjective "Christian" with the noun "Socialism" seems to them out of place. And the reason for this is, that for long both earnest Christians and those who have equally earnestly opposed the Christian religion, have been in the habit of thinking and talking as if "other-worldliness" was the note of a true Christian—as if his main object should be to get to heaven after death. Whereas, on the contrary, so far at any rate, as the teaching of Jesus Christ Himself is concerned, you will find that He said hardly anything at all about life after death, but a great deal about the Kingdom of Heaven, or the righteous society to be established on earth. And as the whole of what I have to say to you depends on the truth of this, I must ask you to allow me to elaborate it to you a little at length.

Christ's significant works.—Take, first of all, that long series of works of Christ's which are generally now called "miracles," but which St. John, at any rate, used to call " signs," significant acts showing what kind of a person Christ was, and what He wished His followers to be; and you will find—without troubling for the moment how they were done, but merely considering what all those who believe they happened are bound to learn from them—that they were all distinctly secular, socialistic works : works for health against disease, works restoring beauty and harmony and pleasure where there had been ugliness and discord and misery ; works taking care to see that the people were properly fed, works subduing nature to the human good, works showing that mirth and joy have a true place in our life here, works also showing that premature death has no right here.   In fact, if you want to point the contrast between Christ and modern Christians, you cannot do better than consider the different way in which He and they speak about premature death.   They are in the habit of saying, when their children die, after their first grief is over, " Oh, it is well with them—they have gone to a better place "; but Christ, so far from encouraging that kind of talk, deliberately, according to the stories which all Christians believe to be true, took pains to bring back into this beautiful world those who had passed off it before the time.   The death of an old man, passing away in his sleep, that, according to Christ, is a natural, an orderly, almost a beautiful thing ; but the death of a child, or a young man, or a man in the prime of life—that is a monstrous, a disorderly thing : not part of God's order for the world, but the result of wrong-doing somewhere or other.   And if you want a rough description of the object of Christian Socialism I should be bold to say that it was to get rid of premature death altogether ; and, when I say that, I am not saying anything absurd or utopian, as you will well understand if you simply compare the death-rate of a poor neighbourhood with the death-rate of a well-to-do neighbourhood, when you will find that even now, while sanitary science is in its infancy, premature death is very largely indeed the result of poverty or of the many evils connected with poverty.

Christ's social teaching.—Turn your attention next to that series of teachings of Christ's which we call parables—comparisons, that is to say, between what Christ saw going on in the everyday world around Him, and the Kingdom of Heaven. If by the Kingdom of Heaven in these parables is meant a place up in the clouds, or merely a state in which people will be after death, then I challenge you to get any kind of meaning out of them whatever. But if by the Kingdom of Heaven is meant (as it is clear from other parts of Christ's teaching is the case) the righteous society to be established upon earth, then they all have a plain and beautiful meaning : a meaning well summed up in that saying, so often quoted against us by the sceptic and the atheist : " Seek ye first the kingdom of God and His righteousness, and all these things shall be added unto you " ; or, in other words, Live, Christ said, all of you together, not each of you by himself ; live as members of the righteous society which I have come to found upon earth, and then you will be clothed as beautifully as the Eastern lily and fed as surely as the birds. Well, we have lived, as you know, on the opposite principle to this ; we have lived on the principle of every man for himself and the devil take the hindermost ; we have lived as rivals and competitors instead of living as brothers, labourer competing against labourer, artisan against artisan, shopkeeper against shopkeeper, trader against trader ; with the result that very few of us are clothed beautifully and many of us not fed surely. Christian Socialists therefore say that it would be worth while to try the experiment, which such an one as Jesus Christ said would succeed, to try and live in a rational, organized, orderly brotherhood, believing that then only, but then most certainly, all the men and women and children of England shall be fed surely and clothed beautifully.

Hell and its inhabitants.—Or look for a moment at two of the parables a little more in detail. Take one of the few parables in which Christ spoke about Hell. For though He did not speak of Hell so much as some of His modern followers do, it is important to bear in mind that

He was not only the Jesus meek and gentle of whom some of you may have sung in your childhood, but also the Jesus stern and angry ; He had His eight woes as well as His eight blessings ; He had fierce denunciations for those who, as He phrased it, devoured widows' houses and for pretence made long prayers ; for those who made the Sabbath day a dull, dreary day by their narrow rules and restrictions ; for those who had the key of knowledge and would not enter into the treasure house themselves, and hindered those who wished to enter in from entering. Yes, even He had language which some superfine people would call outrageous, ungentlemanly, when He sent that message to the king of His country, calling him a jackal—a word of the utmost contempt when we remember that the jackal was the natural scavenger of the Eastern city. We need not be surprised, then, that He who at the right time could be so righteously angry, now and again spoke about Hell.

But who, according to Jesus Christ, was the man who was in Hell ? It was the rich man who was in Hell ; and why was he in Hell ? Not simply because he was rich, for Christ said it was possible, though difficult, for a rich man to enter into His society. No ; the rich man was in Hell simply because he allowed the contrast between rich and poor to go on as a matter of course, day after day, without taking any kind of pains to put a stop to it. That, according to Christ, was the worst state into which it was possible for a man to fall.

What is national righteousness ?—Or take another parable, the parable of the Sheep and the Goats, or the parable of Judgment. In it, if you remember, Christ summoned before His imagination all the nations of the world for judgment ; and it is important to note that it was nations and not merely individuals who were summoned by Christ to judgment ; for you cannot be a good Christian merely by being good in private life, or domestic life : you must be a good citizen in order to be a good Christian : and so it was nations, and not merely individuals, who were summoned to judgment. And what, according to Christ, did the goodness of a nation consist of ? That nation, according to Christ, was good, not which said, " Lord ! Lord ! " most, which was most eager about outward worship or formal religion, but which took care to see that its people were properly clothed, fed, and housed, which looked after those who were in difficulty and distress ; and even in the case of those who said they did not know God, who would call themselves or be called by others Atheists, Jesus Christ said that if they were taking pains to see that the people were properly clothed, fed, and housed, however much they might say that they did not know God, God knew them and claimed them as His. Now, what I have to suggest is that modern English Christians need not presume to be more religious than Jesus Christ was ; and if He said that the 'goodness of a nation consisted in seeing that the people were properly clothed, fed, and housed, then surely it is the bounden duty of every minister of Christ, from the Archbishop of Canterbury down to the humblest Sunday-school teacher, to be doing their best to see that the men, women, and children of England are properly clothed, fed, and housed. I hope, then, that I have said sufficient to make it clear that, so far as Christ's works and teachings are concerned, not only is there no contradiction between the adjective " Christian " and the noun " Socialism," but that, if you want to be a good Christian, you must be something very much like a good Socialist.

The Anti-social Christian answered.—I know, however, that there are two or three sentences of Christ's which are often quoted against this, the whole tone and tenor of His work and teaching. There is the sentence, " Blessed are ye poor " ; the other, " The poor ye have always with you " ; and that passage where, when the younger brother wanted Christ to compel his elder brother to divide his inheritance with him, He said, " Who made Me a judge and divider over you ? Take heed, and beware of covetousness." Let us take this last one first. The younger brother, you will note, was not at all anxious to bring about a general, righteous distribution of wealth ; he was

merely anxious to get into his own possession that which
was then in the possession of his brother : he was for all
the world like those who nowadays are anxious for the
abolition of the laws of primogeniture and entail, but who
take no interest whatever in general righteous social legislation ; and with that kind of thing Jesus Christ said He
would have nothing to do—He saw that mere selfishness
was at the bottom of it ; but He did not on that account
say that He and His followers were not to judge between
the claims of the monopolists and the owners of land-
values on the one side and the industrious people on the
other, and to do all that is possible righteously to divide
the nation's wealth as it is produced amongst those who
produce it.

Or, again, " Blessed are ye poor," said Christ, looking
on the rough, common fishermen and others who were
learning from Him, and comparing them with the Scribes
and Pharisees, the leaders in Church and State, who were
opposing them and Him, and at last got Him killed.   He
said that these poor men, notwithstanding their poverty,
were better and happier men than their opponents ;
and surely we can well understand that that was a true
simple statement of fact ; but that simple statement of
fact gives no kind of sanction to the teaching that has
been drawn from it, that poverty—especially the grinding
poverty which is found in our modern centres of civilization
—is the normal condition of things ; that what the poor
have to do is to put up with their lot here, looking for
a great reward hereafter ; and that what the ministers of
Christ have to do is to teach the poor to be resigned and
submissive here, and to tell them of the rich reward hereafter.   On the contrary, it seems to me to be the duty of
every minister of Christ to do all he possibly can to stir
up a divine discontent in the hearts and minds of the
people with the evils which surround them.   And, once
more, " The poor ye have always with you," said Christ :
" The poor ye shall have always with you," say modern
preachers, and notably the good old Archdeacon of London,
who was called up on a memorable afternoon to preach to
the Socialists in St. Paul's Cathedral.

By the way, it is interesting to remember that on that occasion the Socialists were allowed to go to church without having their banners stolen from them by the police ; and, as they were ranged in front of the west door of their cathedral, I noted that inscribed on those banners and flags there were words taken not from Karl Marx, or Lassalle, or Mr. Hyndman, or Mr. Morris, or Mrs. Besant, or Mr. Champion, or any who were then supposed to be leaders, but taken in almost every case from the sayings of Jesus Christ or His great apostles—so much so that my friend Mr. Hancock shortly afterwards preached and published a sermon, which he entitled " The Banner of Christ in the hands of the Socialists." Well, when these men went into their cathedral they were met by the Archdeacon with words to this effect : No matter, however much you may educate, agitate, organize, you will never get rid of poverty, for Christ has said, " The poor ye shall have always with you." Now, from what I have already shown to you, you will see that, if Christ had said that, He would have contradicted the whole of the rest of His work and teaching ; if He had said that when His kingdom was established—one object of which was to get rid of poverty —there should still be poverty He would have stultified Himself ; but He did not say that, He did not prophesy. He simply said, looking back on the history of His nation, looking round on the then condition of His nation, before His kingdom was established, that He noted the persistence of poverty—a very different thing from saying that there always should be poverty. But even if He had said, " The poor ye shall have always with you," would He have been giving any kind of sanction to the state of things which we see now ? I take it that we are all agreed that, under the best Socialist *régime* imaginable, if a man is a loafer, whether of the east or west, if a man refuse to work when he has every facility and opportunity for working, he will fall into poverty or into something much more disagreeable than poverty. But what is it we see now ? Why, this : that on the whole those who work the hardest and produce the most have the least of the good things of this world for their consumption ; and those who work

very little and produce nothing, or nothing adequate in
return for what they consume, have the most of the good
things of this world for their consumption. So much so
that, as we have been taught, all society at present
can be classified into beggars, robbers, and workers. If a
man is not working for his living, he must either be a
beggar, living on the charity of others, or a robber preying
upon the hard-won earnings of others. And if, again, you
want a rough description of the object of Christian Socialism, I should say that it was to bring about the time when
all shall work, and when, all working, work will be a joy
instead of the " grind " it is at present, and to bring about
the time when the robbers shall be utterly abolished. I
hope, then, you will see that there is nothing in these three
passages, so often quoted against us, to contradict the
whole of the rest of Christ's work and teaching, and that
therefore a follower of Christ is bound to be an out-and-out
fighter against poverty, not merely alleviating its symp-
toms, but getting at the very root and cause of it.

The social teaching of the Early Church.—But
you know that Christ not only worked and taught like this,
but He deliberately founded a society to keep on doing,
throughout the world on a large scale, what He began to
do by way of example, in miniature, in Palestine. He said,
you know, shortly before His death, to those who were to
be the leaders in that society : " He that is loyal to Me
the works that I do shall he do also, and greater works
shall he do." The Christian Church therefore is intended
to be a society not merely for teaching a number of elaborate doctrines—important as they may be for the
philosophical defence of the faith—not even for maintain-
ing a beautiful ritual and worship, important as that is if
men and women are to have all their faculties fully developed, but mainly and chiefly for doing on a large scale
throughout the world those secular, socialistic works which
Christ did on a small scale in Palestine. Now this being so
you would expect to find that the first leaders of the
society, though they would be mainly occupied in founda-
ton work, would have something to say on these secular,

the socialistic questions. Take, for instance, St. Paul; what was his great labour law ? The husbandman that laboureth, said St. Paul, should be the first to partake of the fruits. The labourer is to be the first, not the second, after the capitalist or the third after the landlord, to share the profits resulting from his work. Or, again, St. Paul said, words which it would be well indeed to din into the ears of the Duke of Westminster and the other appropriators of ground values, " Let the robber rob no more, but rather let him labour " ; recognizing that fact of which I have spoken, that if a man is not working for his own living he has preying on the living of others. Or, again, take St. James, who was in such close companionship with Jesus for years. His little pamphlet, which has come down to us through the ages, is full of burning words on the labour question. Take one sentence as a sample, where he says that the cry of the reapers who had been defrauded of their wages had entered into the ears of God, who fights ; that God fought against every law or custom which tended to deprive the labourers of the full reward of their work. And if God so fights, then surely it is certain that it is the imperative duty of every Christian in England to fight against all laws or customs which prevent the workers in England from enjoying the fruits of their work.

The social teaching of the Sacraments.—Or, again, take the two great permanent institutions of the Church, the two sacraments which are universally necessary to salvation—Holy Baptism and Holy Communion ; you will find that they are both entirely on our side. In Holy Baptism, you know, we claim every little baby born into the world as being the equal with every other little baby, no matter whether it be the child of a costermonger or the child of a prince ; not waiting for conversion or illumination, or election or proof of goodness, but simply because it is a human being, we claim it as of right a member of Christ, the child of God and an inheritor— not merely a future heir, but a present inheritor—of the Kingdom of Heaven. The great sacrament of equality is assuredly entirely on our side. And so, too, is the Holy

Communion. The very name tells you that those who
partake of it are bound to live in brotherhood, in fellowship, with one another. There is a hymn sung in church
about having mystic, sweet communion with those whose
work is done ; and those of you who, like rational beings,
have been in the habit of praying for the dead, will know
the value of that communion. But it is even more important to have communion equally mystic and sweet with
those whose work is going on. And that is what this great
sacrament teaches us to have. Indeed, it has been well
said that the real, terrible blasphemer is not the man who
uses foul language at the corners of the street, nor the man
who used to publish those woodcuts in the " Freethinker "
—libels as they were on dead men and a beautiful literature
—but rather the man or woman who says the " Our
Father " morning and evening and takes no kind of pains
to realize throughout the day the brotherhood which that
fatherhood implies, or who comes to the Holy Communion
Sunday by Sunday, month by month, or festival by festival,
and is not striving in everyday life to realize the fellowship
which the Holy Communion implies. Yes, the great sacrament of brotherhood is entirely on our side.

The Catechism and the Magnificat.—Once more, take
the one only document which is binding on all members of
the Church of England, the Church Catechism.[1] You will
find it full of good, sound teaching in the principles of
Christian Socialism. Let me give you one sentence only, a
piece of ethical teaching, which, if it were carried out, would
alter the whole face of English society. It is there taught
that it is the duty which each one—man or woman, rich or
poor—owes to his neighbour, to learn and labour truly to get
his own living ; not to himself, be it noted, in order that he
" may get on "—for you cannot now get on without getting somebody else off—but to his neighbour, that he may
be an honest man. It has been calculated, as you know,
that if all took their share of the work of the world, none
would have to work for more than four hours a day ; that

[1] See the author's " Laws of Eternal Life ;' being Studies in the
Church Catechism." Guild of St. Matthew, 376 Strand, W.C. 3

:he reason why so many have to work under such evil
:onditions and for so long a time is because they have to
)roduce not only sufficient for themselves and their fami-
ies, but also sufficient for a large number of others who
ire themselves producing nothing, or nothing adequate, in
eturn for what they consume. It is against this evil that
)ur socialistic Catechism is aimed. And let it be remem-
)ered that, according to its teaching, it is no kind of excuse
or a man or a woman to say: " True, I do not give back
n return for what I consume anything that I myself have
)roduced, but I give back something which my ancestors
lave produced." To such we say, You eat your own
linners, you wear your own clothes, you require for your-
elf so much house-room ; your great-grandfather can't
at your dinners, or wear your clothes, or use your house ;
.nd therefore, in common honesty, you are bound to give
)ack, not something which your great-grandfather has
)roduced, but which you yourself have produced. And,
astly, think of that Song of Our Lady, the gentle mother
f Jesus Christ, she whom we speak of as not only bright
s the sun, fair as the moon, but also terrible as an army
rith banners. You will find that she has some terrible
rords there. She holds up to the scorn of the ages, as
ests of society, three sets of people—the proud, the
1ighty, and the rich. " He hath put down the mighty
'om their seats " (or dynasties from their thrones), " He
ath scattered the proud ; the rich He hath sent empty
way." No wonder that some of the more far-seeing
ocialists are eager now and again to go to their cathedrals
r parish churches when they have such revolutionary
inguage as that sung to them.

This, then, must be sufficient to indicate to you what is
he religious basis of our Socialism. The work and teach-
1g of Jesus Christ, the testimony of His apostles, of the
wo greatest sacraments, of the Church Catechism, of the
[agnificat—they all surely make it clear that a Christian
i bound to cut right away at the root of that evil which
i the main cause of poverty, and which prevents men
:om living full lives in this world.

The Church and the State.—But at this point I can fancy some of my hearers saying, This is all very well, but if this be true, then the logical result of it is that the bishops in each diocese with their cathedrals, and the parsons in each parish with the churches, should be real leaders and centres of Social Democracy, leading the Church forward to war against poverty; whereas we know that the bishops and clergy, so far from leading, have often tried to hinder all who would help. And though I probably should maintain that there are many more exceptions to the truth of this charge than my hearers would be disposed to admit, I acknowledge the truth of it, and I seek for the cause of it. And there is one reason, at any rate. It is this: that you and your forefathers have allowed the Church to be gagged and fettered; instead of allowing the Church to elect her own bishops and clergy, you have forced them on her from outside. And so now any one rather than the whole body of the parish elects the parish priest; sometimes the landlord, sometimes the bishop, or a builder who wants his villas to let, or a college at Oxford or Cambridge, or a peer, or a jockey at Newmarket; any one, rather than the only people who ought to do it, has the power given them by you to do it. I suggest to you, therefore, by the way, that you cannot expect the Church to live up to the law of her being until you have disestablished and disendowed those whom you now allow to lord it over the Church, and left her free to manage her own affairs. A complete Christian Socialism cannot be brought about until the Church is free to use influence and discipline for the establishment of the Kingdom of Heaven upon earth.

The State as educator.—In the meanwhile much can be done by those churchmen who remember that the State is a sacred organization as well as the Church. They can unite with Socialists of every sort in their endeavour to seize the State and to use it for the well-being of the masses instead of the classes; or, in more prosaic words, they may help to get delegates or deputies returned to Parliament who will carry out the people's will. And therefore for t rest of this paper, having given you what seem to me to be the principles upon which a Christian is bound to be a Socialist, I will touch upon three items on which, in practical politics, we should specially lay stress. And it is important to do this, both because many Christians are somewhat vague in their Socialism, and many Socialists, in my opinion, fail to get at the root of the matter in their joy at getting this or that restriction carried out effectually. First of all, then, we naturally think of the children ; and having got the London day-schools free, we should put forth what energy we can for a liberal expenditure in making them comfortable and pleasant, spending ungrudgingly on such matters as music and swimming ; decreasing the number of children for each teacher, especially in the case of the highest standard and of the exceptionally backward children. We should, of course, also make the continuation classes free, and, further, allow no grant of public money to be given in any form whatever to privately managed schools. These may seem but mild matters to many of the Fabians ; but I cannot help thinking that if our society had been in dead earnest about them last November, the result of the elections would have been different. Of course, it must be frankly stated that these little reforms will not directly tend to raise wages, unless they could be accompanied by general raising of the school age, and then only slightly. While the means of production are monopolized by a few, the reasons for giving the many the best possible schooling are not that it will enable them to get on, but that it will give them the key of knowledge, that it will help to make them discontented, and that it will to some degree teach the value of discipline and inter-dependence. We school them, to a large degree, with this in view, that they may know what is the evil they have to attack and how to attack it. We *do* want to educate them above their station—not, indeed, above that state of life into which it shall please God to call them, but above that into which devilish robbery and monopoly has forced them. Let us once have a generation of young people growing up fairly well educated and thoroughly discontented, and the legal, orderly, social

B

revolution for which some of us are working cannot be long delayed.

The State as employer.—Secondly, in considering their practical political programme, Christian Socialists have to remember, and to remind others, that we are all employers of labour. Now, it is a commonplace of Christian ethics that, while there exist employers and employed, they have duties towards each other. No self-respecting middle-class householder would deny this in the case of his housemaid. What we have to do is to extend the sphere of duty—to get men to understand that, nationally or municipally, they have thousands of servants whom they employ, and to feel that it is their duty to see that these are not overworked or underpaid ; or, in other words, to follow the example set by the late London School Board, and see to it that all those employed by Borough, District, or County Councils, and Parliament are not worked for more than, say, eight hours a day, and are paid the minimum trade union rate of wages. This a Christian Socialist must insist upon, simply as a duty of the delegate of the people to those whom the people employ. If he so treats it, he will not be surprised to find that three years after the duty had, for the first time in English history, been done, those who had benefited by it were so far from being grateful for it that they would not take the trouble to come out on a wet afternoon and vote for those who had got them the benefit. But, further, the people have to remember that no railways, tramways, water-pipes, gas-pipes, wires, etc., can be laid down without their consent ; and that therefore it is their duty, whenever through their various dele-gates or deputies they give that consent, to make as a condition that those who are employed in these various industries should not be overworked or underpaid. This I am urging as a matter of duty from the people to those whom they employ, not as a matter of right on the part of the workers from those who employ them. Duty is a stronger motive power than right ; and it will be time enough for the great mass of the workers to claim their rights from those who employ them when they have dis-charged their duties to those whom they employ. This will involve losing half an hour's wages and running the risk of getting a wet coat perhaps once or twice in three years ; but men who do not care to make that sacrifice in order to discharge their duties are not worth helping in order to get their rights.

Land the mother, and Labour the father, of wealth. —Lastly, I come to what is the main plank in the platform of the Christian Socialist, the chief political reform at which he aims ; being bound by his creed to go to the very heart of the matter ; to be content with no tinkering. It is summed up in the resolution which was moved by the English Land Restoration League in Trafalgar Square, after which the authorities, being Conservative authorities, wisely settled that no more should be said there for the present. It ran as follows : " That the main cause of poverty, both in the agricultural districts and in the great centres of population, is the fact that the land, which ought to be the common property of all, is now mono- polized by a few ; and that therefore those who want to cut away at the root of poverty must work to restore to the people the whole of the value which they give to the land, to get for the people complete control over the land, and to that end see to it that those who use land pay for the use of it to its rightful owners, the people."

Let me make it clear to you how far-reaching will be the evolution worked out by this reform. Let me remind you that if the labourers could get access to the land in the country, even under the condition of paying the same rent per acre to the landlords for a few acres that the farmers now pay for a large number of acres, they would be able, by cultivating those few acres, to get more for themselves and their families than they now get by means of the current rate of wages in the district. This has been proved over and over again by the landlords refusing to let land to the labourers at the same rent per acre for a few acres as they let it at for a large number of acres to the farmers, giving openly as the reason that if they did so wages would be raised. Now, I need hardly remind you that if wages are raised in agricultural labour there is a

tendency for wages to rise everywhere.   Much more, therefore, would the labourers be better off if, instead of paying
rent for those few acres to the landlord, they simply paid
the rent in form of taxation to the State, having to pay
no other taxation whatever.   They would be better off,
not only owing to the relief from taxation, but because the
so-called iron law of wages would then no longer operate;
that law being that while the means of production are
monopolized by a few, wages tend to go down to the minimum at which the workers will consent to live and repro-
duce.   But once get the land, which is the main means of
production, into the hands of the people, and then, instead
of labourer competing with labourer for employment, you
would have employer competing against employer for
labour, which would bring about a very different state of
things.   Or, again, consider what is going on throughout
the agricultural districts.   The labourers by the action of
landlordism are being forced off the soil.   Where do these
men go to ?   Our own experience tells us ;   the Dockers'
Union will tell us ;   the defeated gas stokers will tell us.
It is probably useless and certainly un-Christian for comfortable canons to denounce these men as blacklegs.   The
useful and the Christian thing to do is what Mr. Verinder
and his Red Vans have done, and help to keep them in
the country and there fight landlordism.   For, of course,
you know that, forced off the soil, they crowd into the
already overcrowded large towns ;   there they compete
against the men and women of the towns in their trades
and employments, and so tend to lower their wages ;   and
they compete also for house room, and so tend to raise
rents.   This, I say, is proved by experience, and could b
proved by statistics ;   the population of the villages an
country districts not having increased in anything like th
ordinary normal increase of the birth-rate over the death
rate ;   while the population in the large towns has increase
very much more than the ordinary normal increase of t
birth-rate over the death-rate.   So I have shown to yo
that landlordism prevents wages from being raised, tend
directly to the lowering of wages and the raising of rent
Am I not right therefore in saying that this is the roo

question, the bottom question, which must be dealt with if we want not merely to alleviate poverty by charity, or tinker at it by semi-socialistic trade restrictions, but to get rid of it altogether ?

What makes land valuable ?—But this question can be dealt with, if you like, entirely from the point of view of townsfolk and their rights. If, when discussing the matter, you find that your friend is learned in manures and crops and scientific agriculture, you can for the moment, for the sake of argument, give him in the country altogether, and look at the question solely as the dweller in a large town. I remember, some years ago now, at the Industrial Remuneration Conference, held in Prince's Hall, Piccadilly, presided over by Sir Charles Dilke, that Mr. Balfour was reading a learned paper, in the course of which he said that the land question, however interesting to philosophers and economists, was not a practical question ; for land in England was almost unsaleable. I ventured to interrupt him by asking whether the land on which we were then met was altogether unsaleable. He replied that he was only speaking of land in the country. Well, I have already pointed out to you that if the labourers could get access to it, land in the country would not be altogether unsaleable ; that it may not be well able to support landlord, farmer, and labourer, but that it could well support one man willing to work hard if he was landlord, farmer, and labourer combined. And, by the way, however much men say land is unsaleable, you never find them willing to give away, out and out, one single acre of it. But I say, if you like, you can look solely at town lands. And what do you find then ? Why, you find land in the City of London worth more than £30 per superficial foot ; land in Belgravia worth more than land in Bethnal Green ; land in Bethnal Green worth more than land in Epping Forest. Now what is it that makes the land more and more valuable ? Simply the people living or working in any neighbourhood, or wanting to live and work there. Yet into whose pockets does the whole of this value go ? Not into the pockets of the men

and women who create it, but into the pockets of those
who, often simply because they are the sons of their fathers,
are the owners of the ground rents and values. Robbery
is the only accurate word which a Christian Socialist can
use to describe this state of things.   And there is another
reason why robbery is the only right word to use to describe our present system of landlordism.   It is this : that
land in England used to be held in return for services ; so
much for the army, for the navy, for building bridges,
making roads ; so much for what is now done by means
of the poor laws.   These were the various conditions under
which land was held.   By degrees, however, a Parliament
of landowners and their friends began to shift off from
themselves the responsibility of returning these services to
the State, and began to tax the ordinary articles of the
people's consumption, leaving upon themselves a paltry
tax of 4s. in the pound ; which tax, being assessed not
upon the value which land now has, but which it had
about two hundred years ago, is, I believe, now practically
a tax varying from 1½d. to 2¾d. in the pound.   Now, what
we Christian Socialists urge is that a Parliament of the
people, if they will but take the pains to send honest and
obedient delegates to carry out their will, ought gradually,
but as quickly as possible, to reverse that process ; to take
off all taxation from the articles of the people's consumption, and by degrees to tax the land values, till at last,
taxing them 20s. in the pound, you take the whole of the
land values for the benefit of those who create them.   I
know there are those who maintain that this would do
but little to benefit the worker, because they allege he is
hardly taxed at all at present.   To them, of course, we
reply that, while the main object of the reform is not the
relief from taxation, but to get the land, the main means
of production, into the hands of the people, so that the
iron law of wages might no longer operate, yet practically
the relief from taxation would be important.   For I believe I underestimate it when I say—and this should bring
every frugal housewife on to our side—that if you spend
two shillings on a pound of tea, at least one shilling of that
is tax, or the expense of collecting the tax ; for every

shilling you spend on cocoa, 1¼d. is tax ; every shilling on coffee, 1½d. ; every shilling on currants and raisins, 1¾d. If you spend 3d. on tobacco, a full 2½d. of that is tax ; and if by degrees you spend five shillings on whisky, 4s. 4½d. of that is tax or the expenses connected with the tax. But it is not only the surface of the earth—to which this value, so evidently designed for taxation, is attached by people living and working in any neighbourhood—which the landlords claim, but also the minerals which, in the equally marvellous processes of nature, it has taken centuries to create under the earth : the limestone, the coal, the iron—three things so essential for our great English industries—are claimed by robber landlords. And so, too, the seashore and the rivers ; so that, as Henry George has well said, every salmon which comes up from the sea might just as well have a label on it : " Lord or Lady So-and-So, with God Almighty's compliments."

We Christian Socialists, then, maintain that this is the most far-reaching reform ; that it is demanded by justice ; and not only that it can be carried out in consistence with the highest morality, but that morality is impossible without it.

A peaceful revolution.—Yes, but some one says, this would be all right if you were starting in a new country, but the nation in the past has sanctioned the present system ; it would be destructive of all credit to get rid of landlordism without compensating the landlords. To which we reply that the nation has never given its verdict one way or the other, and that now that it is gradually getting its power to speak it is beginning to be evident what it will say ; and, further, that even if the whole nation in the past had given away to a few people in this generation that without which the whole body of the people cannot live full lives, it would have been doing that which it had no kind of right to do ; that the land of every country belongs of natural and inalienable right to the whole body of the people in each generation ; and, as for compensation, from the point of view of the highest Christian morality, it is the landlords who should compensate the people, not the people the landlords. But practically, if you carry out this reform by taxation, no compensation would be necessary or even possible. We say therefore : " You need not kick the landlords out ; you must not buy them out ; you had better tax them out." And by this process no one will suffer ; land will naturally get into the hands of those who will use it best ; the thrifty artisan who has bought the piece of land on which his house is built will be much better off than he is now if all he has to pay in taxation, local or imperial, is its ground value to the State. The man—say, the borough councillor—who is partly working for his living, and partly living by specu-lating on the wants of others by having bought a street or two of houses, will find that this reform will make it more convenient for him to live entirely by working. The Duke of Westminster and the Duke of Bedford—or rather their children—will be healthier and happier people if they have to take their fair share of the work of the world. Russell Square, if the owners of the houses round have the choice of being rated at what it would let at for building pur-poses, or of opening it to the public, would fulfil the old prophecy, and the gardens of the city would be full of boys and girls playing ; and marriage-hindering Mammon being utterly annihilated, the Alma Venus of Lucretius would again have her way. *Hinc lætas urbes pueris florere videbis.*

Who are the robbers ?—I have now endeavoured to put before you the theological basis of Christian Socialism, and the special political work with which it is concerned. But, although during the last few years there is an in-creasing number of the clergy who are becoming more or less socialistic in their teaching, it would be affectation to pretend that the kind of doctrine I have given in this lecture is the current teaching in the Church at present. In fact, we are often seriously condemned for the line we have taken. It is complained of that we ignore the Eighth Commandment, that we talk about rights rather than duties, that we value material rather than spiritual things. As to the Eighth Commandment, we should indeed be foolish as well as wrong to ignore it, for it is entirely on our side. " Thou shalt not steal " is proclaimed from the altar of West End churches to upper and middle-class congregations, as well as in prison and penitentiary chapels; because the Church recognizes, even though individual clergymen may fail to do so, that it is just as possible— indeed, much more probable—that the rich will rob from the poor as that the poor will rob from the rich. " Thou shalt not steal " is just the commandment we want to get kept; we want to put a stop to the robbery of the poor by the rich, which has been going on for so long. And, as for rights and duties, it is well said that there are no rights without duties and no duties without rights. But we admit that duty is a more sacred thing than right. And I thank my opponents for giving me that word, for it enables me to say, as I have to thousands up and down the country, that it is your bounden duty to claim your rights in this matter. It is not a thing which you may take up or let alone just on the ground that you feel the pinch of poverty or not, but a duty which you owe to yourselves, to your children, to the outcasts from society—to all who are tempted to degrade their lives in any way for the sake of a living. And, more, it is the duty which you owe to God. The earth is the Lord's, and therefore not the land-lord's ; the earth is the Lord's, and He hath given it unto the children of men. And what would any man among you think if he gave to the woman whom he loved some valuable present, and she lightly allowed it to be taken from her ? He would be jealous of the man who got it away ; and so I say that God is jealous when He finds that we have allowed the most valuable of all the material gifts which He has given to His creatures—for " land is the mother and labour the father of all wealth "—to be filched away from us by the Duke of This or Lord That. God is jealous, and we are not doing our duty to God any more than we are doing our duty to our neighbour unless we are doing our very best to prevent this.

The life of the coming age.—And as for material things and spiritual things, I know full well that man does not

live by bread alone. I am as eager for the spiritual welfare of the people as the vicar of this parish or the bishop
of this diocese. I know that it is not only the pasture but
the Presence of which the people have been deprived. But
when they say that because of the importance of spiritual
things we should not turn our attention to these great
material reforms, I wonder whether they have realized the
heredity and environment of a vast mass of the people ;
whether they have considered the evils which result not
only from extreme poverty, but from poverty side by side
with wealth ; how art is now almost impossible, and lives
which should be brimful of mirth and joy are stunted.
Because I take it that when once a man realizes the evils
of our present social state, just because he is eager for the
spiritual life of the people, he will be doing all he possibly can
to put a stop to that robbery which is the main cause of
poverty, and so by degrees to establish the Kingdom of
Heaven upon earth. *Expecto vitam venturi sæculi :* I look
for the life of the coming age.

January, 1892

II. SOCIALISM AND THE TEACHING
OF CHRIST

By the REV. JOHN CLIFFORD, M.A., D.D.

ONE of the objections frequently brought against the
application of the principles of Socialism to our
industrial life is that such a process is opposed to the
teaching and spirit of the Lord Jesus Christ.

Christianity, it is said, moves in a higher realm than
that of humdrum toil, and operates for far higher purposes
than those of settling the disputes of capital and labour,
adjusting profit and loss, organizing production and distribution, fighting a dangerous plutocracy, and mediating
peace between the masses of wage-earners and a narrowing number of wage-payers. It does not "preach a
gospel of material blessedness." It ministers to a mind
diseased by sin, banishes remorse, and prepares for death
and eternity. It is not concerned with this fleeting life, so
brief that "it is like a dewdrop on its perilous way from a
tree's summit," but with the infinite development of the
human spirit through the eternity, and in the home, of God.
In support of this eclipse of the life of the present by the
stupendous and transcendent greatness of the life of the
future revealed in Christianity the saying of Jesus is
quoted : " Work not for the meat that perisheth, but for
the meat which abideth unto eternal life, which the Son
of Man shall give unto you : for Him the Father, even God,
hath sealed."

Hence many Christians look with misgiving on churches
that venture to study the politico-economical conditions of
the life of the people around them, touch with the tips of
their fingers the problems for the abolition of poverty, and

seek the uplifting of the wage-earning classes by juster and healthier modes than those of spasmodic charity and un-limited soup. They denounce ministers who hold and teach that the laws of God run everywhere, even into wages and prices, into houses of toil and the sanitary conditions of factories and drapery establishments; and generally reason that the capacity of the mind for the hospitable entertainment of ideas is so sadly limited that no preacher can be faithful to Christ's message concerning sin and redemption, and at the same time agitate for a "fair living wage," or toil for the reorganization of the industrial life of the country on bases of justice and brotherhood.

Is Socialism Christian?—Professor Flint, a man of vast learning and great ability, has said in one of the largest and least discriminating and most unsatisfactory books I have read on Socialism : " What is called Christian Socialism will always be found either to be un-Christian in so far as it is socialistic or unsocialistic in so far as it is truly and fully Christian " [1]; and, again, " so far as Socialism confines itself to proposals of an exclusively economic and political character, Christianity has no direct concern with it. A Christian may, of course, criticize and disapprove of them, but it cannot be on Christian grounds; it must be merely on economic and political grounds. Whether land is to be owned by few or many, by every one or only by the State ; whether industry is to be entirely under the direction of government, or conducted by co-operative associations, or left to private enterprise ; whether labour is to be remunerated by wages or out of profits ; whether wealth is to be equally or unequally distributed, are not in themselves questions of moment to the Christian life, or, indeed, questions to which Christianity has any answer to give." [2]   To me that is flat Paganism, and as anti-Christian as it is misleading and delusive.

A still more potent voice speaking from the pontifical

[1] " *Socialism.*"   *By Professor Robert Flint ; p.* 441.

[2] " *Socialism.*"   *By Professor Robert Flint ; pp.* 452-3.

chair, Leo XIII, on what are called " socialistic aberra-
tions," asserts their essential antagonism to the Christian
Church ; and the Right Rev. Abbot Snow, O.S.B., goes as
far as to say : " Socialists are led to abolish religion in order
to get rid of its ministers. They (the ministers) are of the
governing class, and let them disappear with the rest.
Thus the process of general levelling and the abolition of
independent authority leads to the negation of religion
and formal worship of God, and makes Socialism tend
to Atheism." [1]
It cannot be doubted that these citations tend to the
widespread feeling on the part of many leisured and comfortably placed Christians, who have had not only the
" promise of the life that now is," but, what is much more,
the splendid fulfilment of the promise : that a league like
our Christian Socialist League has amongst its first duties
to give an account of itself before the tribunal of our Lord
and Saviour Jesus Christ.

The social question.—In doing this let me first of
all fully recognize that these objecting Christians and
churches allow that the Christianity of Christ Jesus is not
averse to the denunciation of the wrongs of modern society
and the exposure of the miseries of our present condition.
Indeed, it is eagerly maintained that Christ condemns every
manifestation of *individual* selfishness, backs every earnest
crusader against *personal* covetousness and greed, and
justifies the strongest language we can use against the
abuses of *individual* competition. All Christians agree in
these outbursts of righteous indignation, and rather enjoy
seeing the vials of oratorical wrath poured out on the
heads of their neighbours ; and some of them are beginning to think that, after all, the " accumulation of gold "
is not the highest virtue, and that there is something
wrong in that medieval interpretation of the words of the
Master, " The poor ye have with you always," which regards the continuance of poverty as a necessary condition
to the exercise of the spasmodic charity of the rich. Many
Christians, if not all, at last admit that there is a social

[1] " *The Catholic Times,*" *August* 10, 1894.

question and that they must do something for it, if it is only to talk about it and to denounce somebody or something. They see the poor separated by a great social gulf from the rich, though geographically not far from one another. They lament overcrowding, and ask what is the chance for chastity and health, for decency and comfort, to say nothing of happiness under such inhuman conditions. Here in West London—in *West* London—is a house of eight rooms and a small ante-room containing not less than forty-two persons ; and it is a sample of the way in which we are violating God's idea of society, and destroying the very germ of social well-being in the extinction of the decencies and wholesomeness of the home. The awful facts borne in upon us by the gathering masses of unskilled, decrepit, and hopeless labourers, the appalling armies of the unemployed, are forcing Christian men to think and to say, " Something must be done." It is not wholly a question of " plenty of room at the top " for the men of tough fibre, clear brain, and iron will ; but of the " strong bearing the infirmities of the weak," and of brother caring for brother. The bitter separation of class from class, the tyranny of drink, the vice of gambling, the debasement and misery of early marriages, the degradation of women, " the huddling together of thousands of workers, the prey of the sweater "—all these increasing wrongs are, it is confessed, inextricably involved in our vast egoistic industrialism ; men, women, and children are caught and crushed in the revolving wheels of this competitive machinery and then flung aside to perish in the workhouse, or to overweight the earlier efforts of their offspring. So that not a few observant souls are ready to accept the strong words of Ruskin and say, " to call the confused wreck of social order and life brought about by malicious collision and competition an arrangement of Providence is quite one of the most insolent and wicked ways in which it is possible to take the name of God in vain." [1]

The sense of spiritual brotherhood.—Some of the disciples of Christ will go further and give personal service.

[1] " *Time and Tide.*" By *John Ruskin ; p.* 9.

A real hearty, loving sympathy carries them to the homes of the poor and suffering, to feed patience, to brighten life, to uphold the afflicted, to sustain the workers in the fierce struggle with toil and want. They believe Christianity bids them preach justice, love, and brotherhood. They even plan for co-operative production. They inculcate stewardship, and bid men to remember that they have to give account of all they have and use to their Father in heaven. To them the social organism is a reality; and the spiritual brotherhood of men more than a phrase. They have seen God in Christ Jesus, and to them the Incarnation is the revelation of their obligations to their brother man, the widening of the definition of sin so as to include transgressions of the parish and city, of the nation and of humanity. No man lives to himself. Cain is anti-Christ. There is a solidarity of man. The kingdoms of this world are to become *the* kingdom of our God and of His Christ. Law and government are not beyond His policy; and even our industrial civilization may be shaped according to His will. It is a great change; and those who have experienced that regeneration of the social consciousness in the churches of Christ are shaping the future of labour and of the life of the world.

Where Christians part.—But it is when we come to a *social policy*, to a *method* or industrial rearrangement, that the question arises whether we are moving along the lines of Christ's ideas, and are providing *the best industrial body for the incarnation of His spirit.* It is at this third stage we part. Christian men are agreeing more and more: (a) in their antagonism to individual greed and injustice; (b) in personal and sympathetic devotion to the welfare of the people; the parting of the ways is (c) as to the real basis on which modern industry shall organize itself. It is when scientific Socialism or Collectivism says: (a) Our industrial life should be based not on individual but on a collective ownership of the chief elements and material instruments of production; (b) that production should be managed not according to the will or caprice or might of private individuals, but collectively; and (c) that the results

of toil should be distributed to all who have a share in th
toil on the principles of absolute justice, i.e. on the princi
ples of equality in value;[1] it is then we are charged witl
opposing the teaching of the Master.

Now, let there be no mistake as to what this Collectivisn
is. It does not advocate the absorption of the individual
by the State; or the suppression of the family; or the
total extinction of private property; or the direction of
literature, and art, and religion by the collective wisdon
of the community; it does not involve the sudden over
throw of the machinery of industrial life; but in the light
of the historical development of industry it seeks to accele-
rate the evolution of the industrial life, so that it shall free
itself from the defects and evils that now belong to it, and
shall fulfil its Divine mission in the enrichment of the
whole life of mankind. It seeks to build a far better body
for the soul of Christ's teaching, and the spirit of His life
and death, than this fiercely competitive system, through
which He now struggles almost in vain to make His voice
heard and His power felt.

The possibility of Collectivism.—I may take it for
granted that our present industrial *régime* is not final.
Collectivism is at least *possible*. It is often forgotten that
the present commercial system is not far advanced. It
has scarcely travelled through its earlier and more crude
years. There is no fixed necessity for regarding the present conditions of production and distribution of wealth
as their final form. The era of Individualism, of syndi-
cates and companies, of capitalists sitting round a green
table and directing the movements of hundreds of labourers
with no connection with each other except that created by
what Carlyle calls the "cash-nexus," may give place to
one in which State-industrialism, as seen in our police
arrangements, post-office, the civic ownership and control
of gas, water, electric lighting and tramways, Government
employment of labour in Woolwich and Portsmouth Dock-
yards and Enfield factories, enforcement of education, and

[1] *" Socialism : its Nature, Strength, and Weakness."* By
Professor R. T. Ely ; p. 9 *et seq.*

ιe payment of teachers for the children of the nation, the
:ovision by the rates of public baths, wash-houses, parks,
ιrdens, art galleries, museums, hospitals, and asylums,
ill issue in a completely equipped co-operative common-
ealth. All these may be. Human nature is confessedly
ery intractable ; but British society may pass by certain
:ages from the limited Collectivism which now exists to
ιe which covers the whole machinery of the lower part
[life, and provides for that physical basis of human exist-
ιce on which the spiritual structure is being slowly reared.
Mr. Robert Wallace, M.P., told us in a magazine article,
The Collectivist scheme can never be set up." He did
ot think " the private capitalist will allow himself to be
estroyed." No doubt the said capitalist will strenuously
ᴣsist his extinction, and he may be successful, though that
ι not very likely, considering the massive strength and
remendous energy of the social forces now at work. But
he *practicability* of Collectivism is not our question. We
ssume that what Mr. Hayes, in his story " The Great
ᴕevolution of 1905 " calls " the ideal of common sense,"
ιay be " applied to the business transactions of the
ιation," and that the " very simple organization " of
:ollectivism may be substituted for the existing chaos of
omplexity, stupidity, and inefficiency, and utterly hope-
ᴣss failure to meet even the most elementary requirements
ιf a civilized community.

What Collectivism would do.—Asserting, then, that
here is nothing in Christianity against the change, and
ιssuming that it is not impracticable, I now seek to prove
hat the Collectivist arrangement has at least four distin-
ιuishing merits, demonstrating its closer and stronger
ᴑfinities with the teaching of Jesus Christ than the present
ᴅethod of administering the physical life of man : (1) It
ᴅestroys the occasions of many of the evils of modern
ᴑciety ; (2) it advances, elevates, and ennobles the struggle
ᴑf life ; (3) it offers a better environment for the develop-
ᴅent of Christ's teaching concerning wealth and brother-
ᴅood ; and (4) it fosters a higher ideal of human and
ᴑcial worth and well-being. I do not deny all ethical

ι C

advantage to the individualistic system. I am aware
has developed that prodigious business capacity in
limited and distinguished few of our workers which s
cured to Britain thirty years ago the commercial prima
of the globe. It has created the race of merchant prince
traders, and paragons in developing and supplying ne
material wants. It has found the opportunity for builde
of enormous industries in coal and iron, in the productio
of food and clothing, of machines and news, thereby brin
ing the produce of the world to our doors and the news
the world to our tables. It has fed legitimate ambitio
and saved men from indolence, quickened the sense
responsibility, educated, drilled, and enriched inventiv
and business faculty.

Not for a moment would we forget these advantages
but we cannot bind ourselves to the fact that, as a system
it has not stirred the most unselfish desires nor fostere
the most generous sympathies on any large scale. It h
been egoistic, not altruistic. It is more in keeping wit
the gladiatorial than the Christian theory of existenc
It provides for ruthless self-assertion rather than sel
restraint. It does not inspire brotherly helpfulness, bu
the crushing of competitors and thrusting aside of rival
Instead of co-operating in the struggle to save and enric
the lives of others, it tends to make its administrators fo
getful of their claims, and renders it necessary to bring th
power of legislation to the support of children in coal-min
and factories, to the protection and defence of weak wome
to the limitation of hours of labour, and the imposition
sanitary conditions of toil. Could any confession be
stronger indictment of individualistic views of labour que
tions than John Morley's, in his *Life of Richard Cobde*
" Modern statesmanship has definitely decided that u
fettered individual competition is not a principle to whi
the regulation of industry may be entrusted." It is a fa
that pure individualism gives every advantage to th
strong and renders no aid whatever in bearing the infirm
ties of the weak. If that is in the least bit in accordan
with the mind of Christ, then I must confess that I hav
failed to read aright its wonderful contents.

On the other hand, Collectivism, although it does not change human nature, yet it takes away *the occasion for many of the evils which now afflict society*. It reduces the temptations of life in number and in strength. It means work for every one and the elimination of the idle, and if the work should not be so exacting, responsible, and, therefore, not so educative for a few individuals, yet it will go far to answer Browning's prayer :—

> " *O God, make no more giants,*
> *Elevate the race.*"

Hesiod teaches that " Work is the one road to excellence." ' There is no shame in labour ; idleness is shame." An effortless existence is intolerable, and leads to incalculable mischief. Individualism adds to the number of the indolent year by year ; Collectivism sets everybody alike to his share of work, and gives to him his share of reward.

As it is necessary to work, so it is useless to steal. Misrepresentation is not a gain. Grasping avarice is " out of work." Equivocation lacks opportunity. Crimes against property are diminished, and become more and more rare. The degradation of woman ceases in so far as it is due to want. The problem of the " unemployed " is solved. And the possibilities of realizing a nobler type of manly life are increased a thousandfold. Surely all this is in perfect harmony with the teaching and spirit of " Him who came to seek and save that which was lost."

The elevation of the struggle for life.—Another sign of the closer kinship of Collectivism to the mind of Christ is *in the elevation and nobility it gives to the struggle for life*. Collectivism does not extinguish combat, but it lifts the struggle into the worthiest spheres, reduces it to a minimum in the lower and animal departments, and so leaves man free for the finer toils of intellect and heart ; free " to seek first the Kingdom of God and His justice." Benjamin Kidd says : " True Socialism has always one definite object in view, up to which all its proposals directly or indirectly lead. This is the final suspension of that personal struggle for existence which has been waged, not only from the beginning of society, but in one form or another from the beginning of life." But I think that Professor Drummond puts the matter more completely, and there-fore more fairly, when he says : " War is simply the modern form of the struggle for life. As the higher quali-ties become more pronounced and their exercise gives more satisfaction, the struggle passes into more refined forms. One of these is the industrial struggle. Another is the moral struggle. The former of these must give place to the latter. The animal struggle for life must pass away. And under the stimulus of ideals man will continually press upwards, and find his further evolution in forms of moral, social, and spiritual antagonism."

It is a fact " as soon as the first wants are satisfied, the higher wants become imperative." Engrossed in the " things that are on the earth," man cannot seek the things that are above. Chained sixteen hours a day to the car of labour, his life is one of toil and sleep ; an animal life almost of necessity. But Collectivism secures leisure for the cultivation of character ; man is not so fretted and worn by the exhausting use of his bodily facul-ties that there is not strength as there is not opportunity for the higher labour of spirit on behalf of the life that is life indeed ; but he is as fresh as he is free, and so the dis-placing of the animal from the throne of existence is at least rendered possible, where now it can only be accom-plished, if accomplished at all, in the face of tremendous odds. Labour is thus brought into accord with the Greek idea of the state ; and, like it, exists " not for the sake of life, but of a good life." Are not these results in keeping with " the mind of Christ " ?

The ideals of labour and brotherhood.—Again Collectivism affords a better environment for the teach-ings of Jesus concerning wealth and the ideals of labour and brotherhood. If man is, according to Drummond, only " the expression of his environment," if, indeed, he is that in any degree, then it is an unspeakable gain to bring that environment into line with the teaching of Jesus Christ.

In the Gospels accumulated wealth appears as a grave peril to the spiritual life, a menace to the purest aims and the noblest deeds. Christ is entirely undazzled by its fascinations, and sees in it a threat against the integrity and progress of his kingdom. "Lay not up for yourselves treasures on earth." "Man's life consists not in the abundance of the things he possesses," but in the *use* he makes of what he has—if for himself—still for himself, not as an end, but as a means for promoting the well-being of the world. Jesus frowns on the hoarding of wealth. Collectivism renders that accumulation unnecessary and inconvenient. Still, Collectivism does not mean confiscation. It is not robbery. The Bishop of Derry is reported to have said that the spirit of Socialism says : "Here is a man who possesses more than we do ; let it be taken from him." Whereas that of Christianity says : "Here is a man who has less than I have ; let me give him something." "Socialism" is a vague term, I admit, and probably there is somewhere a "socialism" that speaks the language attributed to it by the Bishop of Derry ; but that is not the speech of scientific Socialism or Collectivism. It says : "Here is the great business of industrial life ; let us manage it so that all may share in the responsibility and share in the gains, and share fairly and justly as nearly as possible ; not one doing all the work and another taking all the gains." It is allowed that individualism in commerce affords abundant opportunity for the use of wealth. It creates means for splendid charities. The millionaire can feed the hungry, clothe the naked, and heal the sick. He can build cathedrals, endow universities, give libraries for study and parks for recreation. And he has done it. Abundant are the witnesses to his wisdom and goodness in distributing his wealth for the welfare of the people, and large is the contribution to the progress of the world due to his thoughtful generosity. But it is some drawback to this consideration that the means for philanthropic work are placed exclusively in the hands of a few ; and that the *occasions* for it are due, not only to the vices of men—drunkenness, gambling, and the like—but also in a large measure to the political, industrial, and social injustices of the reign of individualism. For we must ask : How are these fortunes made ? Have any neighbours' landmarks been removed ? Is there any grinding of the faces of the poor ? Are the workers doomed to harsh and hard conditions of toil ? It is notorious that our individualistic commerce is often a tyrant where it should be a servant and an injustice where it ought to be a help. Here is a picture drawn by Frederic Harrison :—

"Ninety per cent of the actual producers of wealth have no home that they can call their own beyond the end of the week ; have no bit of soil, or so much as a room that belongs to them ; have nothing of value of any kind, except as much old furniture as will go in a cart ; have the precarious chance of weekly wages, which barely suffice to keep them in health ; are housed for the most part in places which no man thinks fit for his horse ; are separated by so narrow a margin from destitution that a month of bad trade, sickness, or unexpected loss brings them face to face with hunger and pauperism. And below this normal state of the average workman in town and country there is found the great band of destitute outcasts—the camp followers of the army of industry—at least one-tenth of the whole proletarian population, whose normal condition is one of sickening wretchedness. If this is to be the permanent arrangement of modern society civilization must be held to bring a curse on the great majority mankind." (Report of Industrial Remuneration Conference, 1886, p. 429.)

Now, though Collectivism does not profess to extinguish vice and manufacture saints, it will abolish poverty, reduce the hungry to an imperceptible quantity, and systematically care for the aged poor and for the sick. It will carry forward much of the charitable work left to the individual initiative, and, like the London County Council, provide recreation grounds, adding the charms of music for adults and gymnasia for the children. Again, I ask, is not all this in harmony with the spirit and teaching of Him who bids us see Himself in the hungry and sick, the poor and the criminal ?

The Christian conception of industry.—Possibly

ιe greatest gain of Collectivism is in its stronger affinity
ith the high ideals of individual and social life given by
hrist Jesus. Collectivism fosters a more Christian concep-
on of industry ; one in which every man is a worker, and
ιch worker does not toil for himself exclusively, but for
ιe necessities, comforts, and privileges he shares equally
ith all the members of the community. He works for
hat we call " the State," i.e. for the whole of the people
[the city and nation in whose prosperity he has a direct
ιterest and whose business is carried on for the welfare
[all his fellows, and thereby for himself ; succouring the
eaker members, aiding the aged and infirm, and reclaim-
ιg those who are vicious and criminal, as part of the duty
[a collectivist citizen.

It is to the pliant genius of Greece we owe the first
fort to reconcile the claims of the State and of the indi-
idual. The Greeks were gifted with the power of delicate
ιdgment, of combining principles apparently opposite, of
armonizing conflicting claims ; they possessed a sense of
ιeasure, a flexibility, a faculty of compromise opposed to
ιe fatal simplicity with which the Eastern politics had
een stricken. Not tyranny nor anarchy satisfied the
reek, but " ordered liberty." [1] It is that ordered liberty
hich obtains in and through the collectivist arrangement
[human industry, ruling out fierce competitions and
ιethodizing the struggle for the life of others ; making the
ork for bodily living automatic and regular and unex-
ιausting to the last degree ; and so securing leisure for
ιe larger life of the mind and heart, of the imagination
nd of the spirit.

It is notorious that the ideals of individualistic labour
re narrow, low-roofed, and self-centred, and men neither
ave time nor chance to win " their soul," the Divine
ortion of their life and of the life of society, the life of
oble aims, tender humanities, strong faith, and glowing
ιve of God and of men.

It is a new ideal of life and labour that is most urgently
ιeeded. England's present ideal is a creation of hard

[1] *Cf. Professor Butcher, " Some Aspects of the Greek
ιenius " (52 et seq.).*

individualism; and therefore is partial, hollow, unreal and disastrous. But ideals are the main factors in the progress of the home, the parish, and the State. They are the forces that move individuals. Individualism fosters the caste feelings and the caste divisions of society, creates the serfdom of one class and the indolence of another; makes a large body of submissive, silent, unmanly slaves undergoing grinding toil and continuous anxiety, and a smaller company suffering from debasing indolence and continual weariness; begets hatred and ill-will on one hand, and scorn and contempt of man on the other. No! the ideal we need and must have is in the unity of English life, in the recognition that man is complete in the State, at once a member of society and of the Government—"a ruler and yet ruled"; an ideal that is the *soul* at once of Collectivism and of the revelation of the brotherhood of man in Jesus Christ our Lord, Son of God and Son of man.

Finally, I am sure that as we seek to build up our industries more and more on this basis we shall discover that we need a deep and widespread revival of the Spirit of Christ, a clearer insight into His ideas, so that we may suppress the passions that feed our individualistic system and sweep away the accumulated evils which have gathered round it, and at the same time to advance to perfection the Collectivist methods already operative in profit-sharing, in co-operative labour, and in municipal and State indus Collectivism will become an argument for a deepened s life. Were we more Christian we should, as di the n Christians, seek with passionate ardour to incarnate a collective rather than an individualistic idea in society. Nothing more forcibly witnesses to the need of Christ than the failure of the churches to cope with the evils of nineteenth-century life. It is Christ we need. Light both leads and kills. Science has just told us the swiftest and surest foe of the disease-spreading germs is the light. Christ is the light of the world. He shows us the way we should take; and He also will yet destroy the microbes of physical and moral pestilence and death in our modern industrial life, and render the animal the obedient servant instead of the tyrannical master of the human spirit.

February, 1895.

III. SOCIALISM AND CHRISTIANITY

By THE REV. PERCY DEARMER, M.A.

*" I seriously believe that Christianity is the only founda-
tion of Socialism, and that a true Socialism is the necessary
result of a sound Christianity."*

FREDERICK DENISON MAURICE, 1849.

IT is extraordinary how little many Christian people
realize the meaning of their own religion, so that they
are actually shocked very often at Socialism ; and yet all
the while Socialism is doing just the very work which they
have been commanded by their Master to do. This fact is
so obvious that no representative and responsible Christian
body can be found to deny it.

Take as an example of this the most representative
official English religious gathering possible—the Pan-
Anglican Conference of Bishops which met at Lambeth
just twenty years ago. These prelates, drawn from all
parts of the world, belonging by birth to the propertied
classes, by station to the House of Lords, and by tradi-
tion to the Tory Party, made a solemn pronouncement
on the subject of Socialism. Here, if anywhere, we
should find a denial that Socialism was Christian. But no !
They turned and blessed it. Here are the words of their
Encyclical :—

" The Christian Church is bound, following the teaching
of her Master, to aid every wise endeavour which has for
its object the material and the moral welfare of the poor.
Her Master taught her that all men are brethren, not because they share the same blood, but because they have a

common heavenly Father. He further taught her that if any members of this spiritual family were greater, richer, or better than the rest, they were bound to use their special means or ability in the service of the whole. . . . It will contribute no little to draw together the various classes of society if the clergy endeavour in sermons and lectures to set forth the true principle of society, showing how Property is a trust to be administered for the good of Humanity, and how much of what is good and true in Socialism is to be found in the precepts of Christ."

The next Conference, that of 1897, endorsed this view and, in fact, distinctly strengthened it.

So, then, in 1888, when there was no *Clarion* and no Labour Party, we parsons were told in the most solemn way by our official leaders that we were to be social reformers, to preach the Brotherhood of Man, and to show " how much of what is good and true in Socialism is to be found in the precepts of Christ." In writing this tract, therefore, I am but obeying the instructions of my Fathers in God.

An old agricultural labourer once admitted to me that Socialism was " all backed by Scripture "; and I need hardly remind any one who reads his Bible that if I were to put down every passage that makes for Socialism, I should want a pamphlet several sizes larger than this. But nothing is more futile than the unintelligent slinging of texts ; and I shall therefore confine myself strictly to the *central features* of Christianity, and not pick out chance sayings here and there, since that could be done with the writings of every great moral teacher that has ever lived. Christianity is different. It does not only provide a few noble sayings that Socialists would welcome. It *is* Socialism, and a good deal more.

And because I have only space for the central features of the Christian faith, I must pass over the magnificent utterances of the Old Testament prophets and confine myself to the strictly Christian documents, and in these to the sayings and doings of Christ and His Apostles, with a reference to some leading principles of the Church universal.

How Christ came.—How did Christ come into the world ? That is the most important point of all, the most central. We Christians believe that God the Son became man. He could have come in any class He chose, and the Jews expected the Messiah to appear as a great Prince. If Christ had come thus, as an Oriental potentate, in pomp and luxury, with a crowded harem and troops of soldiers, the influential Jews of the day would have welcomed Him. But He was born in a stable. He came as a working man. He worked at His own trade till He was thirty : and then, choosing other working men as His companions, He tramped about the country as one that had not where to lay His head ; doing innumerable secular works of mercy, besides preaching spiritual regeneration ; and blessing the poor, while He condemned the rich and denounced the proud teachers and leaders of the national religion ; and, after three years, He was executed by the law of the land, because He preached revolutionary doctrines, which the common people " heard gladly," but which were detested by the religious authorities of the day.

This was not only a reversal of all that the Jews expected, but it was also a new phenomenon in the world's history. No one before had ever thought of setting on such a basis the message of social regeneration. Nay, even the noblest of Greek philosophers, the constructors of ideal States, had utterly failed to take account of labour, and had based their ideal republics upon slavery. To Plato even the masses had but " half a soul " ; while Aristotle, who regarded slaves as " living machines," and women as nature's failures to produce men, wrote : " Certainly there may be some honest slaves and women ; nevertheless it may be said that woman generally belongs to an inferior species, while a slave is an utterly despicable being " '(" Polit." i. 13). And in Athens, B.C. 309, the slaves are said to have numbered 400,000 out of a total population of 515,000.

But by the Incarnation not only was labour given its true position, but the unity of the whole human race was proclaimed. Humanity in its solidarity was taken upon Himself by the Divine Word, and every human being declared to be an infinitely sacred and precious thing, with transcendent rights to the fullest development.

Everybody knew it.—Nor was there any doubt about it from the first. Christ's Mother knew it as soon as she knew that He was to be born of .her ; and she sang that revolutionary hymn, the *Magnificat*, which is still, curious to relate, repeated every day at Evensong in church : " He hath scattered the proud in the imagination of their hearts, He hath put down the mighty from their seats, And hath exalted them of low degree. He hath filled the hungry with good things, And the rich He hath sent empty away " (Luke i. 51–3). And at His Nativity there was a similar demonstration of social fellowship as inseparable from true religion : " Glory to God in the highest," the angels sang, " Peace on earth ; Goodwill among men."

The man who was sent as Christ's forerunner, to prepare the way before Him, knew it also. " Every valley shall be filled," he cried (Luke iii. 5), " and every mountain and hill shall be brought low," putting the *levelling* principle in a nutshell. And when the people asked him what they ought to do, he just told them to practise communism : " He that hath two coats let him impart to him that hath none, and he that hath food let him do likewise " (Luke iii. 11, R.V.). Is it not just what Socialists are trying to do— to level up the valleys, to scatter the proud, to fill the hungry by an equal distribution, and to change an un-Christian state of society, under which it is the *poor* who are sent empty away ?

The first public utterance of our Lord Himself pro-claimed the same social revolution. On that solemn occa-sion when He began His mission, He went into the Syna-gogue at Nazareth ; He took the roll of the Hebrew Scriptures, and, out of all the sayings therein, He chose this one : " The Spirit of the Lord is upon me, Because He anointed me to preach good tidings to the poor : He hath sent me to proclaim release to the captives, And recovering of sight to the blind, To set at liberty them that are bruised, To proclaim the acceptable year of the Lord " (Luke iv. 18, R.V.). Could anything be more significant ?

Wanted, orthodoxy.—And now I come to the question, What did Christ Himself teach ? He taught much about God, but He also taught much about men. Religion has these two sides, and both are of immense importance. Let it be clearly understood. This tract is not written to belittle the Godward side of religion, or to condone that lack of spirituality which is too common already. But its subject is the duty to our neighbour, which is as much neglected as the duty to God.

It is noteworthy in this connection that the great Pagan writer, Lucian, was as much struck by the social as by the theological side of the new religion. In the passage where he notices the existence of Christianity, he remarks : " It was impressed on them by their original lawgiver that they are all brothers, from the moment that they are converted. . . . All this they take quite on trust, with the result that they despise all worldly goods alike, regarding them merely as common property." Lucian's ' Works " (H. W. and F. G. Fowler's translation), vol. iv. p. 83.

Now, we hear, and we need to hear, a great deal about our duty to God ; but how about that other duty which our Lord declared to be " like unto it "—the duty to our neighbour ? The Church Catechism teaches all its little children that it is just as imperative to love our neighbour as ourself as to love God. And surely what we have to show Christian folk is not that we want them to embrace some strange new form of Christianity, but that we want them to be faithful to the old ; not to give up their faith, but to hold it in all its fullness ; not to be unorthodox, but to be really orthodox—orthodox about this duty to their neighbour, which St. John, the most profoundly spiritual of all the Bible writers, declares to come before the duty to God : " For he that loveth not his brother whom he hath seen, how can he love God whom he hath not seen ? " (1 John iv. 20).

What, then, was the social teaching of that Man, who came to reveal God to men, and yet whom St. Peter described afterwards (Acts x. 38) as one who " went about doing good " ? We will take the four most prominent

forms of His teaching—His Signs, His Parables, His
Sermon, His Prayer.

Christ's signs.—Very often when we go into church we
find the congregation singing some hymn which expresses
the utmost weariness of life and the keenest desire to die
and pass to the " better land." Stout old gentlemen and
smart young women sing it lustily ; and we know that
they are singing a lie ; for if they were told that they were
to die to-morrow they would not find it at all weary
" waiting here." That is an instance of the heresy of
modern popular religion. Christ taught exactly the opposite. The vast majority of His miracles restored men to
health and life, and enabled them to go back to their work,
and to enjoy the measure of life which God allots to mankind. Death in old age, when a man's work is done, is not
a sad thing ; but death in youth, or in the prime of life,
is piteous, horrible, abnormal ; and so are sickness and
deformity.

Christ, then, devoted a large portion of His time to
fighting against disease and premature death, and He wept
when a friend had been carried off in his prime. St. John
always calls these " miracles " (as the word is mistranslated
in the Authorized Version) by the name of *signs*—that is,
significant acts. If we, then, realize their significance, if
we are imitators of Christ in this, too, according to our
power, we shall heal sickness, and fight against disease and
death, in the workshop and in the slum dwelling ; since all
sanitary and social reform is but carrying out on a larger
scale the signs which our Lord wrought for our example.
" He that believeth on Me, the works that I do shall he
do also ; and greater works than these shall he do ; because I go unto the Father " (John xiv. 12). For instance
of the children that are born in the working classes, about
one-half die before they are five years old—according to
Dr. Playfair, fifty-five per cent as against eighteen per cent
among the rich. And yet, if we even offend or despise
one of these little ones, He tells us (Matt. xviii.) it were
better for us that we were cast into the sea with a mill-
stone about our neck ! It is surely no empty form that

to the most respectable congregations it is said from the
altar Sunday after Sunday, " Thou shalt do no murder."
For we are all sharers in this ghastly holocaust, and the
blood is on our hands, unless we are labouring with all our
power to prevent it.

But, further, we learn from the signs of Christ not only
to save life and health, but to increase its comfort, as He
did at the feeding of the multitudes—and its merriment, as
He did at the Cana marriage feast.

Christ's parables.—Many of the parables too, deal with
social questions. Many are terrific attacks on money-
making, and one was the inspiration of that epoch-making
treatise on economics, Ruskin's *Unto This Last*.
Another was commonly supposed to be difficult only because people did not see that money, the " Mammon of
unrighteousness," must be used so as to make *friends* of
men ("Make to yourselves friends *by means of* the mammon," Luke xvi. 9, R.V.) and not enemies—a Socialist
moral, as Archbishop Trench himself explained in his
standard work on the parables.

Another, that of the Good Samaritan, it is very necessary to remember for this reason : that it gives an entirely
new meaning to the word " neighbour." When the Jew
said, " Love thy neighbour as thyself," he only meant
' Love thy people," thine own tribe, as was taught in the
Old Testament (" Thou shalt not avenge, nor bear any
grudge against the children of thy people, but thou shalt
love thy neighbour as thyself," Lev. xix. 18). But when
Jesus, in answer to the question, " Who is my neighbour ? "
Luke x. 29) told the story of the Good Samaritan, He expressly showed that He meant by neighbour every human
being all the world over, including " enemies " even. Now,
as there is no other reference to the Golden Rule in the
Old Testament but this one in Leviticus, which confines it
to relations, it is not really true to say that our Lord, in
saying, " Love thy neighbour," etc., and " Do to others,"
etc., was only repeating an Old Testament maxim. It
was, as He said, " a new commandment " : " A new commandment I give unto you, That ye love one another "

(John xiii. 34). Maundy Thursday owes its name to this
novum mandatum, or new commandment. The three chap-
ters of this Great Discourse (John xiii. to xvi.) should be
carefully studied.

And here I would point out the meaning of a whole
series which are called the " Parables of the Kingdom."
They expressly confute the common notion that the Kingdom of Heaven is something only in the next world, and
that men are set only to save what Kingsley called " their
own dirty souls." For these parables are quite unintelli-
gible unless we believe that our Lord came to found a great
human brotherhood, a kingdom which He called His
Church, here on the earth. He came expressly to found
this society, of which the New Testament is so full ; He
came thus on a social mission to bind men together in love,
as well as to purify their individual souls. And so He said
that this " Kingdom of Heaven " was like a draw-net
(Matt. xiii. 47), not consisting only of converted persons, but
of every kind ; and like a field (xiii. 24) where the tares and
wheat grow together; like a grain of mustard seed (xiii. 31)
in the way it should grow; and like leaven (xiii. 33), which
should spread till it had made the whole world good.

But the last parable He ever uttered is the most important of all, because in it He told men by what they were
to be judged at the Last Day. If we know how we shall
be judged, then we know what we have to do—how we are
to be true Christians. And what does this great Parable
of the Judgment (Matt. xxv. 31–46) tell us will settle our
fate in the next world ? Extraordinary to relate, it is just
the opposite to what the professedly religious world has
been saying, and just the very thing that the Socialists
teach. We shall be saved or condemned according to our
acts of social service, Christ tells us, saying nothing about
church-going, or conversion, or orthodoxy ; for these latter
are nothing unless they are so genuine as to have a practical
result. " Faith without works is dead " (James ii. 14–26).
We shall be placed on His right hand if we have fed and
clothed and helped others—not merely among our own
friends, for sinners do that (Luke vi. 32–4), but those who
cannot help themselves ; and our Lord, in a magnificent

passage, asserts the solidarity of all mankind in Him by identifying Himself even with the poor wretch in an unspeakable Eastern prison. Then, turning to those on His left, He says : " Depart from Me, ye cursed, into the eternal fire," not because you were heathens or agnostics, but because " I was an hungered and ye gave me no meat : I was thirsty, and ye gave me no drink : I was a stranger, and ye took me not in ; naked, and ye clothed me not ; sick and in prison, and ye visited me not. . . . Inasmuch as ye did it not to one of these least, ye did it not unto Me." St. Basil, in his Homily on Riches, shows the feeling of the early Church about this parable when he says : " The robber is not even arraigned [at the Day of Judgment], but the unsocialist [*ho akoinonetos*] is condemned [*katakrinetai*]."

Christ's Sermon.—And this great principle, that what we do is of far more importance that what we profess, is made the clinching passage of the Sermon on the Mount Matt. vii. 16–26) : " By their fruits ye shall know them. Not every one that saith unto Me, Lord, Lord, shall enter into the Kingdom of Heaven, but he that doeth the will of My Father." What that Will is we shall see further on. But here I will point out how this sermon directly contradicts modern individualism, both secular and religious.

Our religious individualism is condemned in three prominent characteristics—its self-righteous censoriousness ' Judge not. . . . Thou hypocrite, first cast out the beam ut of thine own eye "—vii. 1–6) ; its parade of " charity," falsely so called, and subscription lists (" But when thou doest alms, let not thy left hand know what thy right hand doeth : that thine alms may be in secret : and thy Father which seeth in secret shall recompense thee "—Matt. vi. -4, R.V. Not " Shall reward thee *openly*," which is a late addition by some scribe, who hankered after antithesis, and so destroyed the real point) ; its love of cant (" And when thou prayest, thou shalt not be as the hypocrites are : for they love to pray standing in the synagogues and in the corners of the streets "—vi. 5, 6).

And now for what the sermon says about secular individualism. Here are the Beatitudes, with which the

D

sermon begins, printed by Ruskin side by side with their modern perversions :—

CHRIST.	PRESENT-DAY.
Blessed are the poor in spirit : for theirs is the Kingdom of Heaven.	Blessed are the rich in flesh : for theirs is the Kingdom of Earth.
Blessed are they that mourn : for they shall be comforted.	Blessed are they that are merry ; and laugh the last.
Blessed are the meek : for they shall inherit the earth.	Blessed are the proud : in that they *have* inherited the earth.
Blessed are they which do hunger and thirst after righteousness (*dikaiosuné*, justice) ; for they shall be filled.	Blessed are they which do hunger and thirst after unrighteousness (injustice) in that they shall divide its mammon.
Blessed are the merciful ; for they shall obtain mercy.	Blessed are the merciless, for they shall obtain money
Blessed are the pure in heart : for they shall see God.	Blessed are the foul in heart : for they shall see no God.
Blessed are the peacemakers : for they shall be called the children of God.	Blessed are the war makers : for they shall be adored by the children o men.

To which one might add two further parallels to the two remaining Beatitudes :—

Blessed are they which are persecuted for righteousness' sake : for theirs is the Kingdom of Heaven.	Blessed are those who persecute the lovers of justice : for they prevent the Kingdom of Heaven.
Blessed are ye, when men shall revile you, and persecute you, and shall say all manner of evil against you falsely for My sake.	Blessed are ye, when the Press shall speak well of you and praise you ; for so did their fathers to the false prophets.

It is worth noticing that St. Luke, in the first Beatitude has simply ' the poor," and follows immediately with

"Woe unto you that are rich"; and scholars think that St. Luke gives the original which was modified by St. Matthew. (See, e.g., *The Study of the Gospels*, by the Dean of Westminster, pp. 76 *ff*.) "Poor in spirit," of course, does not mean poor-spirited, but simply the not caring about private property. Poverty in Christ's time *did not imply pauperism or degradation*, but such a simple life as the fishermen-apostles lived.

Besides this, the following principles are also taught in the Sermon on the Mount : Love of our enemies, anger being a form of murder (Luke vi. 27; Matt. v. 21-44); affirmation instead of oaths ; avoidance of capital punishment, and of all litigation and retaliation (Matt. v. 33-41); a warning that we are not to insist on the "rights of property" (v. 40) ; a command to give to every one that asks our help (v. 42) ; a command to lend without asking interest or even the principal back (Luke vi. 34, 35) ; the wrongfulness of all forms of "making money" (Matt. vi. 19-20) ; and the consequent impossibility of serving God if we serve Mammon (vi. 24) ; that "thrift" is not the right way to abolish poverty (vi. 25-34). But that God wishes all men to have good food, and drink, and beautiful clothes (vi. 29-32), without either the grinding worry of poverty or the deadening lust of riches (vi. 24, 31, 34) ; and that this happy state of things is to be obtained by our seeking, first of all, two things—the holy brotherhood and the justice of God. "Seek ye first the Kingdom of God and His righteousness, and all these things shall be added unto you" (vi. 33). Seek ye first the divine society and the divine justice, and all these things—clothes more beautiful than Solomon's, and good food and drink—shall be added unto you. Be social, godly, just, and you shall have Utopia. But the modern world is anti-social, selfish, unjust, and we have—London !

It may be urged that some of these precepts of the sermon are ideal, and not practicable under present conditions. This is true. But it proves that a social system under which the precepts of Christ cannot be carried out is not a system which Christians can be content with. Christianity is, in fact, far ahead of us ; and we have to assist in developing society in the direction of this ideal. So far as we can see, that direction is also the direction of Socialism ; although as man develops from his present rudimentary condition to the glorious future which evolution and the Gospel alike foretell, he may pass beyond the ideal of present-day Socialism to something vaster and more sublime.

Christ's prayer.—A prayer is generally considered a particularly " other-worldly " thing, or, at least, when it is concerned with this world, it is nearly always selfish and limited, like the prayers children are taught—" Bless father and mother, and make Tommy a good boy," which curiously illustrates how general is the narrowing of modern religion, and grows naturally in after years to—

> *Bless me and my wife,*
> *My son and his wife,*
> *Us four and no more. Amen.*

Our Lord gave us only one prayer, and that quite short, for He set it as a model on which all prayer was to be based. How far we have departed from that model will be clear if we consider its clauses one by one.

The Lord's prayer was originally given for private use : " But thou, when thou prayest, enter into thy closet, and when thou hast shut thy door, pray to thy Father which is in secret " (Matt. vi. 6). Here, then, if anywhere, we shall find Individualism ! Let us see. The prayer contains seven petitions and three extra clauses. *None* of these ten parts are individual ; *all* are social, three of the petitions are distinctly what some people would call " worldly," while the three extra clauses are specially inserted to insure the social application of the rest.

OPENING CLAUSE.—" Our Father which art in heaven." At the very outset Individualism is renounced ; though we pray " in secret " we have to say " Our," and to include all humanity in our prayer, approaching God as the common Father of the whole human family. And no one can say " Our Father which art in heaven " unless he has first said " Our brethren which are on the earth,"

1ST : PETITION.—" Hallowed be thy Name." The first petition, like the two next, refers to this world. There should be no full-stops between this petition and " In earth as in heaven." In Westcott and Hort's Greek Testament, which represents the high-water mark of biblical scholarship, the clauses are thus printed :—

> *Our Father which art in heaven :*
> *Hallowed be thy name,*
> *Thy kingdom come,*
> *Thy will be done,*
> *In earth as in heaven :*

How, then, is God's Name to be hallowed here upon the earth ? Certainly not by a state of things under which in London alone, according to Mr. Charles Booth (*Life and Labour*, ii. 20–1), 1,400,000 people are living in want ! If blasphemy in word is wrong, how about blasphemy in deed ? Whenever we make any earthly matter the mirror of the love and justice of God we are hallowing His Name, for we are vindicating His righteousness ; but where is the love or justice in modern trade, or politics, or diplomacy ? Ask a City man, and he will reply, with a smile, that business is business ; by which he means that selfishness must be supreme, untinctured by any thought of mutual love or justice. Indeed, a few years ago, before the Socialist protest, every political economist would have told you that men can only be reckoned with as ' covetous machines." Now, this is the real blasphemy, the real atheism and materialism. It has driven thousands of working-men into revolt against God, because they felt they could not believe in a loving Father when they saw the blank misery and oppression all around them. Yet God made the country, God places man amid lovely surroundings, which are the glory and delight of poet and artist ; and man, modern commercial man, has made the hideous modern town, which shuts out every ennobling influence from those who have to live in it. In fact, it is generally admitted by the most conservative people that the devil made the town "—that prince of jerry-builders !

To hallow God's name, then, we must make the world a mirror of His love and beauty and justice.

2ND AND 3RD PETITIONS.—"Thy Kingdom come, Thy will be done." God has given man free-will because it is better to be free and imperfect than to be an irreproachable machine. But God's evolution of the world is towards perfection. Therefore Socialists are right in believing in Utopia ; and as Christians we are bound to be Utopians. People often object that we are dreamy, unpractical people, because we are idealists. But every one who says the Lord's Prayer definitely proclaims himself a fellow-worker with God for a perfect social state ; he prays for a heaven on earth, for God's will to be as perfectly done here as it is in heaven, for men to be as perfect as the angels, and for this divine evolution to take a social form in the " Kingdom of God." He is *bound*, then, to believe that all our struggles for social and moral reform are leading us to a Utopia. As Ruskin says : " When you pray ' Thy Kingdom come,' you either want it to come or you don't. If you don't, you should not pray for it. If you do, you must do more than pray for it—you must live for it, and labour for the Kingdom of God."

, 2ND EXTRA CLAUSE.—" In earth as it is in heaven." Our Lord inserts this to make it quite clear that He does not mean us to use the three foregoing petitions in an unreal or other-worldly sense.

4TH PETITION.—" Give us this day our daily bread." When it is evening, and the day's work is over, you are still bound to say this prayer ; for it is morning on the other side of the earth, and there are hungry people in the Antipodes. When your larder is full, you must use it none the less ; for it is not " Give me," but " Give us." And is not " Give me my daily seven-course dinner and champagne," but " Give us our daily bread." Here, in the short prayer, Christ yet found room for a thorough statement of our most mundane needs—necessities for *all*, but harmful luxuries for no one. If, then, a rich man uses this prayer, he is morally bound to distribute his excess from his luxury to supply other men's necessities, and labour for a more equal distribution of wealth. For what

one man has another cannot have, and every penny one
man has above the average product of society forces some
one else to have less, and perhaps to lack his " daily
bread."   On this point we may compare Luke iii. 11,
already quoted on page 44 : " He that hath two coats,"
etc. ; James ii. 15–17, R.V. : " If a brother or sister be
naked, and in lack of daily food, and one of you say unto
them, Go in peace, be ye warmed and filled ; and yet ye
give them not the things needful to the body ; what doth
it profit ?   Even so faith, if it have not works, is dead in
itself " ; and also 1 John iii. 17 : " But whoso hath the
world's goods," etc., quoted on page 59.

5TH PETITION.—" And forgive us our trespasses."   Well,
you may say here, at least, is something that has nothing
to do with Socialism !   Hasn't it ?   Look again.

This also has an EXTRA CLAUSE attached to it, so care-
ful was our Lord to guard against Individualism—" as we
forgive them that trespass against us."   Here, even here,
then, the Christian Faith is social, corporate, reciprocal ;
and as we shall be judged by our treatment of our brother,
so by our conduct towards him we are forgiven.   Christ
never allows us to get away from this neighbour of ours.
Therefore it was only to be expected that modern heresy
should have raised a cry directly the opposite of Christ's
principles.   " No man shall come between me and my
God," is that cry—as if they would make private property
even of the Almighty !   But the teaching of the Lord's
Prayer is that *every man* shall come between me and God.
God will not even forgive us, unless we " forgive our
debtors."

6TH PETITION.—" Lead us not into temptation."   It
may be objected that nothing so far has been in favour of
economic Socialism, of State Collectivism.   That is quite
true ; for if our Lord had taught economics, instead of
religion with its two great duties, He would never have
led the world to brotherhood at all : all real economic and
legislative reform has been the *effect* of moral regeneration ;
can never be its cause.   True Socialism is a much larger
thing than Collectivism, which is but the means for realizing it under present conditions.   As Bishop Westcott

says : "The method of Socialism is co-operation, the method of Individualism is competition. The one regards man as working with man for a common end, the other regards man as working against man for private gain" (*Socialism*, by B. F. Westcott, late Bishop of Durham, p. 4. Price 1d. C.S.U. Pamphlets, No. 3. Mowbray and Co., 34, Great Castle Street, London, W.). Thus, when humanity has established Collectivism, it might very possibly pass on to Communism ; and, after some centuries of Communism, humanity might become pure enough to live without laws at all, which would really be Anarchism. Christ taught for all time ; and, if He had insisted on Collectivism, men would never have become unselfish enough to attain it ; if they had, His teaching would have grown out of date. But His teaching and His example are always in advance of us, and thus we are able to develop.

But it is clear to my mind that this 6th Petition teaches us to be Collectivists at the present stage of the evolution of society. "Lead us not into temptation." Clearly if we twentieth-century folk were Anarchists, we should be living in overwhelming temptation ; and if you and I, my Socialist friend, were living as Communists, I am afraid we should find that Tom, Dick, and Harry, not to mention Levi and Cohen, would be tempted to take advantage of us. But the State in which we do happen to live is Individualistic, and I need hardly remind you that under this present competitive system the atmosphere of temptation is terrific. In the office and the workshop, in the studio and behind the counter, all day long the voices cry : "Make money, honestly if you can ; but, at all events, make money ! If you want to get on, you mustn't mind shouldering So-and-so out of the way. You must look after Number One. Every man for himself, and the devil take the hindmost ! "

Now, I think this, more than anything else, has made me a Socialist. I know that money is the main cause of the awful temptations of these modern times, which have seriously made a new gospel, not of good-will towards men but of "Self-help" ; and I want not only to be freed from this temptation myself, but I want " us " to be freed from

it, for I know that it is destroying all our nobility of character. If I want, then, mankind not to be led into
temptation, I cannot support the present competitive
system. Only one means of escape can I see, and that is
to destroy material competition, which every page of the
Bible condemns, and to establish, so far as possible, the
collective ownership of the means of production, distribution, and exchange. We cannot at present do away with
money in some form, although we are told that money is
a root of all evils (1 Tim. vi. 10, R.V.). But we can, by
putting money into the common purse, minimize the temptation till humanity is ready for a further step. Thus are
we to apply to our present conditions the eternal principles
which Christ gave us, and which He gave just that we
might apply them from age to age, till God's will is perfectly done and the whole lump is leavened. Can any one
produce a better way of doing this than State Socialism ?
If not, then let us be State Socialists.

LAST PETITION.—" But deliver us from evil." Unsocial
Christians have to learn from this how much of the evil is
social, of " the world," as the New Testament so often says,
using the word " *cosmos*," which means in the Greek " the
order of the world," just as we say " the present social
system." And Materialistic Socialists have to learn that
it is Evil from which we have to be delivered. Nothing is
so shallow as to think that our social disorder is due to
economic machinery which can be altered without any
change in men's hearts ; that is just the stupid materialism
of the old political economy turned inside out. Our disorder is due to the evil which made this machinery ; it
continues because there is so much evil that men tolerate
this machinery. Our statute-book is what it is because
men are what they are : Socialist Acts of Parliament are
only passed as men become more social ; and some of the
best of those Acts are a dead-letter to-day because men
are too selfish to enforce them. When there is less evil in
the world, less of that original sin for which the modern
name is Individualism, then, and not till then, will the
Parliament which *we* elect, and the autocrats which Slav
and Teuton working-men hold upon their thrones, allow

Socialism to be established. You cannot, it is most true, make humanity good till you have made its environment good ; but it is also true that you cannot make that environment good till you have made men better. The two must improve each other. And the perfect State will consist of perfect men and women.

Having now some idea of the drift of Christ's teaching, let us consider a little more fully the two leading principles of Socialism—Brotherhood and Common Wealth—in the light of the whole New Testament.

Brotherhood.—I need hardly dwell on this. Every Christian admits it—in theory—and would be surprised if the parson addressed his flock as " ladies and gentlemen " instead of " brethren." We only have to make Christians true to the religion they profess, and to have the same religion for week-days as for Sundays. We only have to make the respectable church-goer understand that it is really devilish to stand aloof from those whom he may think beneath him, since St. John says that " In this the children of God are manifest, and the children of the devil : whosoever doeth not righteousness is not of God, neither he that loveth not his brother " (1 John iii. 10).

The pity of it is that many a professing Christian does not know anything about this brotherly love. He forgets that he has to love his brother as *himself ;* and so the very word " charity " has lost its true meaning, and is even applied to those petty forms of almsgiving which may justly be called the crumbs that fall from the rich man's table.

What we falsely call " charity " the New Testament call ALMSGIVING, and our Lord, the first time He mentions it calls it *justice* (Matt. vi. 1, R.V.). And yet, when some on cries, " We want justice and not charity," we think he i proclaiming a brand-new Socialist doctrine ! The rea CHARITY is described at length by St. Paul (1 Cor. xiii. as something that " seeketh not her own," but is patient kind, generous, modest (v. 4), courteous, good-tempered guileless (v. 5), honest and sincere (v. 6), confident an brave (v. 7). And this virtue is proclaimed by St. Pau as the greatest thing in the world, greater even than faith and hope—two virtues, by the way, which are almost equally necessary for the social reformer. Further, St. John says of this virtue (our translators for some extraordinary reason translated it " love " in St. John, but it is the same Greek word) that if we dwell in it we dwell in God Himself (1 John iv. 16), and that " every one that loveth is born of God and knoweth God " (iv. 7), while "he that loveth not" (however much he goes to church) " knoweth not God." And it is remarkable that while St. John includes the love of God in this Charity, he expressly describes it as a social virtue : " But whoso hath the world's goods, and beholdeth his brother in need, and shutteth up his compassion from him, how doth the love of God abide in him ? " (iii. 17, R.V.). He expressly declares that God is Love, and yet this Divine Love is analysed by St. Paul as made up of acts of love *to men*.

As the inspired William Blake wrote—

> " *Love seeketh not itself to please,*
> *Nor for itself hath any care,*
> *But for another gives its ease,*
> *And builds a heaven in hell's despair.*"

There is another virtue necessary to brotherhood, which is a watchword with Socialists. It is JUSTICE. You may not think that it occurs often in the Bible. But it does occur eighty-six times. For every time you find the word ' righteousness " you may read for it " justice." The word in the original Greek is *dikaiosuné*, which means justice, and is so translated in the Latin Vulgate by *justitia*. No doubt " righteousness " had a much broader sense originally, and should mean more than " justice " instead of less ; but it has been degraded, like the word Charity, by modern use. Remembering this, observe that our Lord spoke of " the unrighteous Mammon," that is, of riches, as an unjust thing ; that He said, " Blessed are they which hunger and thirst after Justice."

Every Socialist knows that a main offence against brotherhood is *Idleness*, and he claims that every idler is

in fact a criminal. St. Paul is with him : " If any will
not work, neither let him eat " (2 Thess. iii. 10, R.V.) ; work,
he says, in another place (1 Thess. iv. 12), " that ye may
walk honestly," being unable to conceive of an honest idler.
The Communion Service, too, is with him : " Six days
shalt thou labour," with a provision for a weekly holiday.
The Catechism is with him : " My duty to my neighbour
is . . . to learn and labour truly to get mine own living,
and to do my duty in that state of life unto which it *shall*
please God to call me." Not " has pleased to call me,"
as it is generally misquoted. The Catechism does not say
that men should be kept down, but that wherever the
young may find themselves in after-life they are to do their
duty. And Jesus Christ gives no invitation to the idler :
" Come unto Me, all ye that *labour*."

How miserably insincere we are, by the way, about that
great religious provision for a weekly holiday ! Pious
shareholders and directors, who would be shocked at their
own children playing some innocent game on a Sunday,
will yet deprive the railway men of their one day in the
week—for the sake of money. And the ratepayers cheer-
fully put their police on duty for a seven-day week, because
otherwise they would have the expense of a larger police
staff to maintain. A man cannot always have Sunday,
but he can always have an equivalent day, if his employer
will maintain a proper number of men.

There is a Socialist song which tells of the time when
there shall be " no master " ; and here again they can
quote our Lord's own words : " One is your Master, even
Christ," " and all ye are brethren " (Matt. xxiii. 8, 10).
" Ye know that they which are accounted to rule over the
Gentiles lord it over them ; and their great ones exercise
authority over them. But it is not so among you : but
whosoever would become great among you, shall be your
servant : and whosoever would be first among you, shall
be bond-servant of all. For verily the Son of Man came
not to be ministered unto [waited upon], but to minister "
(Mark x. 42–5, R.V.). It has been rather stupidly objected
that St. Paul was in favour of slavery because he told
servants to obey their masters. But we have only to re-

ember that the early Christians were so full of the spirit
f revolt against the " world " or society under which they
ved that they often had to be held back from ruining
e whole cause by disorderly conduct. They knew that,
ey were free, that God was no respecter of persons (Acts
. 34), and that however respectable a man was, if he ap-
roved of class-distinctions, he was " guilty of all " sin
[ames ii. 1-10). See especially vv. 5-9, R.V.: " Did not
od choose them that are poor as to the world to be rich
faith, and heirs of the kingdom which he promised to
em that love Him ? But ye have dishonoured the poor
an. Do not the rich oppress you, and themselves drag
ou before the judgment seats ? Do not they blaspheme
e honourable name by the which ye are called ? How-
eit if ye fulfil the royal law, according to the scripture,
ou shalt love thy neighbour as thyself, ye do well : but
ye have respect of persons, ye commit sin."
Therefore St. Paul, who was famous as a man that had
turned the world upside-down " (Acts xvii. 6), had to
ell them that nevertheless they must stick to their work.
his is also true of the early Fathers. They drew a dis-
nction between " natural law " and " human law." They
ll agreed that both private property and slavery were not
accordance with natural law, being due to man's sinful
ondition ; but they held that they were justifiable under
uman law. At the same time they taught that to give
p both private property and slaves was a good deed, and
ey set the example of doing so themselves. (See A. J.
arlyle, *Mediæval Political Theory in the West*, and Pro-
ssor Nitti, *Catholic Socialism.*)
St. Paul took pains to point out that the Christian slaves
rho were as churchmen on a perfect equality with the
trician Christians) were to do their service, " not to
en," but " as to the Lord " (Eph. vi. 7) ; and he repeats
is when he writes to the Colossians : " Servants . . .
atsoever ye do, do it heartily as to the Lord, and not
men. . . . And there is no respect of persons " (Col. iii.
-5). What St. Paul taught when he wrote to a master
y be read in his little letter to Philemon, which is an
eal to a master to receive back a runaway slave, but " not

now as a servant, but above a servant, a brother beloved"
(Phil. 16). And, as a matter of history, wherever the
Church has been, she has emancipated the slaves and
vindicated the dignity of womanhood.

If we try for a moment to apply the law of Christian
brotherhood to our present conditions, it is clear that they
cannot stand for one moment before it. All monopolies
would go, all class-distinctions would go, and war would
be no more. Society would become Socialist, for we are
not to lay up treasures *for ourselves* upon the earth (Matt.
vi. 19), we are each to labour, and not to take interest
upon capital (Luke vi. 34, 35)—interest being the great
modern means of obtaining money without working for
it—we are not to maintain our own rights of private pro
perty (Matt. xix. 21 ; 2 Cor. ix. 9 ; Luke xii. 13–21), but
are to work in complete co-operation and harmony one
with another (1 Cor. xii.). We are to love our neighbour
as *ourself*, to vote for his interests as our own, to educate
his children as we would like our own educated, to fee
his wrongs as wrongs done to us—in fact, as an early
Christian writer says, " both to work and pray to get him
all the good things we have ourself " (St. Justin Martyr
Tryphon, 95). We are to do to him as we would have him
do to us were our places changed ; and " *this* is the law
and the prophets " (Matt. vii. 12). That goes much
further than the Socialist maxim : " Each man counts a
one, and no man as more than one."

Thus, if our brother is poor, we must labour for his
release from the grinding, harassing toil which shuts out
from him the higher things of life.

Ah ! but if he is rich, you say, ought we not to con
gratulate him on his prosperity, and regard his property
rights as sacred ?

Common wealth.—Pardon me, my friend. If you are
a Christian, and love your rich neighbour as yourself, you
will do all you can to help him to become poorer. For
you believe in the Gospel, you know that to be rich is the
very worst thing that can happen to a man. That, if
man is rich, it is with the greatest difficulty that he can b

saved ; for " it is easier for a camel to go through the eye
of a needle, than for a rich man to enter into the Kingdom
of God " (Mark x. 25).   This is startling now, but it was
not less strange and startling to the disciples, who " were
astonished out of measure, saying among themselves, Who
then can be saved ? "   But the needle's eye has not grown
any larger since then, and the camels certainly have not
grown smaller !

Certain very superior persons, even among Socialists,
have blamed Jesus Christ for so often denouncing the rich.
But this is just wherein He showed His wisdom.   It was
a perfectly new idea at the time ; for even the disciples,
who were not rich, were shocked.   But after hearing it for
nineteen hundred years, Christendom still acts as if it were
peculiarly difficult for a *poor man* to enter the Kingdom.
And as we look round at both Church and Nonconformist
governing bodies, boards of management, and representative assemblies, or at their clergy—bishops, priests, and
deacons, Dissenting ministers and pastors—we find, as a
matter of fact, that the poor man *is* excluded, and that
the rich have somehow or other all squeezed through the
needle's eye, and have comfortably taken over the direction of the poor man's Kingdom !   And the State is worse
than the Church ; it was pointed out a few years ago that
in democratic America every member of the Cabinet but
one was a millionaire.   Can we blame, then, our Lord for
putting the case so strongly, since even now it has not
yet been driven into our greedy heads ?   As a matter of
fact, the undesirableness of riches is the hardest lesson for
man to learn ; and he *has* to learn it, if Socialism is to be
established on mutual love, or, for that matter, if it is to
be established at all, because otherwise it is impossible.

How strongly our Lord enforced the lesson I need not
remind you.   People sometimes try to get out of the
Parable of Dives and Lazarus by calling it the Parable of
the Bad Rich Man.   It is not ; it is the Parable of the
Rich Man.   Old-fashioned Bibles give it the title of " The
rich Glutton," which shows how our grandfathers shut
their eyes to its meaning.   They might as well have called
t " The rich Dandy " ; and, indeed, there is nothing about

gluttony in the parable, the words translated "fared sumptuously" being better rendered by "living in mirth and splendour," as in the R.V. margin.

Dives was an ordinary person, who was not without the ordinary good-nature of the selfish, for he at least allowed Lazarus the hospitality of his doorstep ; whereas nowadays we should send at once for the policeman if Lazarus attempted such a thing. We are told why Dives was punished in Hades : "Son, remember that thou in thy lifetime receivedst thy good things, and likewise Lazarus evil things" (Luke xvi. 25).

St. Augustine well says on this point : "Jesus said not, a calumniator ; He said not, an oppressor of the poor ; He said not, a robber of other men's goods, nor a receiver of such, nor a false accuser ; He said not, a spoiler of orphans, a persecutor of widows,—nothing of all these. But what did He say ? *There was a certain rich man.* And what was his crime ? The Lazarus lying at his gate, and lying unrelieved."—Augustine, *Serm.* clxxviii. 3.

All true Christians, then, must desire to relieve the rich man of his excess for his own sake, since the inequality that ruins the body of Lazarus ruins the soul of Dives ; and Dives is the more miserable of the two, because the soul is more precious than the body.

St. James perfectly understood this great truth that the social revolution will be really a blessing for the rich. He stated it in the clearest terms : "Let the brother of low degree rejoice in that he is exalted : but the rich, in that he is made low : because as the flower of the grass he shall pass away" (James i. 9, 10). This passage, by the way, happens to be the special Epistle for May 1st, which is St. Philip and St. James' Day, and therefore it has been read throughout the Church on every Labour Day for about 1,500 years. It is still bound to be read every May Day. Outside, the Socialist procession may be singing the reactionary Marseillaise, but in church the reactionary vicar is reading to his people the Socialist message of St. James ! It is a wonderful world we live in.

The identity of true Socialism with true Religion is nowhere more clearly shown than in the Christian teaching

about riches. The great rival power to God is not any of
the common bugbears of the religious world—not heathen-
dom, or popery, or the public-house, or the theatre—but
Mammon. If, then, we are fighting against the power of
riches, we are essentially Christian. " Ye cannot serve
God and Mammon " (Matt. vi. 24 ; Luke xvi. 13). And
St. Paul makes it still clearer when he says (Col. iii. 5) that
idolatry, the worship of a rival to God, is covetousness.
The common religious notion of idolatry is that it consists
in putting up graven images in church ; but the New
Testament has given the word a different meaning—it is
the worship of the graven image upon a coin. Covetousness is now so openly professed that the economists have
built a science upon it ; yet St. Paul more than once
mentions it as an equally disgraceful thing with nameless
vices ; to take a milder instance, he says (Eph. v. 5) :
" No whoremonger, nor unclean person, nor covetous man
who is an idolator hath any inheritance in the Kingdom of
Christ." And covetousness was the sin of Judas.

.Once more, I repeat it. If the love of money is a root
of all evils (1 Tim. vi. 10), we can only make the people good
Christians by making the State the common trustee, which
shall pay us all justly for work duly done ; " not looking
each of you to his own things, but each of you also to the
things of others " (Phil. ii. 4, R.V.).

The Christian Church.—What did the first Christians
do when their Church was settled in Jerusalem ? They
lived as Communists ; this Communism was, indeed, voluntary. " Whiles it remained, was it not thine own ? "
(Acts v. 4). They shared out of their own free will, because they felt that it was the right, Christian thing to do ;
and this makes it more significant than if it had been forced
upon them. They must have known what the Master
really meant ; they had heard Him speak, and knew
thousands of sayings of His which have not come down
to us (John xxi. 25) ; they had the apostles amongst them,
and had not the divine teaching on hearsay. " And the
multitude of them that believed were of one heart and soul :
and not one of them said that aught of the things which

he possessed was his own ; but they had all things common " (Acts iv. 32, R.V.). And as a natural result of this
Communism (as St. Chrysostom reminded his hearers many
years afterwards) " great grace was upon them all. For
neither was there among them any that lacked : for as
many as were possessors of land or houses sold them, and
brought the prices of the things that were sold, and laid
them at the apostles' feet : and distribution was made
unto each according as any one had need " (Acts iv.
33–5, R.V.). From each according to his ability, to each
according to his need !

Thus we have reached from the first proclamation of a
levelling revolution to the establishment of a deliberate
voluntary communism co-extensive with the first Church.

My task is nearly done. I have only now to point out
that this Church is still pledged to Christian Socialism, not
only by her first documents, but by her history. The
Communist experiment at Jerusalem failed, which was
significant as showing how intense was the conviction of
those who tried it so long before the time was ripe. But
the Church did not give up the Socialist ideal for that.
Note, for instance, how Tertullian (200 A.D.) appeals to
the Socialism of the Church as a thing which can be taken
for granted, and which excites the wrath of the pagan
world : " And they [the pagans] are angry with us for calling each other brethren. . . . The very thing which commonly puts an end to brotherhood among you [pagans],
viz. family property, is just *that* upon the community of
which *our* brotherhood depends. And so we, who are one
in mind and soul, have no hesitation about sharing our
possessions with each other."—Tertullian, *Apol.*, 39.

If, indeed, the Church had given up her Christian
Socialism, then Christ, who promised to be with it even
to the end of the world, would have been wrong. There
have, indeed, been plenty of bad bishops, and bad priests
and people, and periods of corruption and recovery ; but,
all along, the leaven has been working, and the kingdom
growing nearer and clearer—aye, even amid the deluge of
modern avarice. Nor can any one who has studied the
slow processes of evolution in man and nature approve for

one moment the ignorant objection that nineteen hundred years is a long time to have taken. It is a short period in the world's history. And all along the corporate Church, as distinguished from individuals, has consistently maintained the same ideal. A form of Communism, confined to religious orders because it could not be practised in the world, has never ceased to flourish ; it has always been held up as an ideal life, and whenever people wanted to be particularly good they have, as a matter of course, lived a communal life, following Christ's advice : " If thou wilt be perfect, go and sell that thou hast, and give to the poor " (Matt. xix. 21). At the present day hundreds of thousands of Christians are so living.

   It was the Church in early days, as the Bishop of Birmingham has shown, that invented representative government (C. Gore, *The Mission of the Church*, p. 143 ; *The Church and the Ministry*, pp. 97-107). The Church also steadily condemned *all* receiving of interest on capital down to the sixteenth century, and canon law still bears witness to this in theory. There are, indeed, two great economic doctrines which were not only preached, but enforced by the Church courts and accepted by all business men down to the age of the Reformation. One of these was the prohibition of interest. The other was the doctrine of the " just price," which said that a man was not to ask what he could get for a thing, but was to demand only the just price, viz. what it ought to fetch in order to enable the maker of it to lead a decent life according to a recognized standard. These were not mere pious opinions, but were principles universally practised ; and thus for 1,500 years the " selfish machine " of modern economics was not allowed to exist. (See Professor Ashley's *Economic History*, vol. i. chap. 3 and ii. 6.)

   All those whom the Church delights to honour, the Fathers and the saints, from St. Matthew to the author of the *Utopia*, have practised and preached some form or other of what we now call Christian Socialism. Many of the sayings of modern Socialists are, indeed, but echoes of what is to be found in the Fathers. For instance, Proudhon's famous saying that " Property is Robbery " was anticipated 1,600 years ago by St. Ambrose : " Nature therefore created common right, Usurpation made private right " (*De Off.* i. 28).

In her sacraments she has constantly proclaimed the sacredness of common earthly things ; in Baptism she asserts the absolute right of every human being, however young, or poor, or ignorant, to her brotherhood.   Indeed St. Paul, in his splendid comparison of the brotherhood (1 Cor. xii.) to the one body with many members, wherein if one member suffer all the members suffer with it, bases his whole contention upon this sacrament of Baptism. " For in one Spirit were we all baptised into one body, whether Jews or Greeks, whether bond or free " (1 Cor. xii. 13, R.V.).

In the Holy Communion she has maintained the communal character of the highest form of worship ; for, as the *Didachè* said in the second or third century (iv. 8), following the still earlier *Epistle of Barnabas* (cxix. 8) : " If you are sharers in the imperishable things [i.e. communicants], how much more must you be sharers [communists] in those things that are perishable " ; " therefore thou shalt not turn away from him that hath need, but shalt share all things with thy brother, and shalt not say that anything is thine own."   This is just what so shocked people when Mr. Stewart Headlam said that those who come to Holy Communion must be holy communists.

By her very existence the Church declares the solidarity of the human race and its essential unity, free from all distinction of class, sex, or race, " neither Jew nor Greek, bond nor free, male nor female, for ye are all one man in Christ Jesus," as St. Paul insists in three separate epistles (Gal. iii. 28 ; Col. iii. 11 ; 1 Cor xii. 13).

Much of all this has been forgotten, since Christians have devoted all their energies to breaking up the Church into competitive sects, and fighting with each other, and have made an apotheosis of selfish individualism by the Calvinistic heresies of justification by faith without works, the impossibility of falling from grace, and the still more hideous doctrine of predestination.   I simply ask Christians of all kinds to be true to their common mother, the historic Church, and not be misled by those who have overlaid her teaching with their own selfishness. And to those who are not conscious Socialists I say, Why not ? Have you any reason except a selfish one ? Why hold back and be half-hearted ? You and we are at one. For Christianity is not Individualism. Neither is it Socialism and water. It is Socialism and fire—the practical religion of those whose inspiration is " comfort, life, and fire of love."

And to those Socialists who are not consciously Christian I also say, Why not ? You are serving Christ. You and we are at one. We are fighting against the same evils. Look at our devotional books, and you will find at the beginning the ancient tabulated lists of virtues and vices. You will see that we love the same things that you love—Justice, Love, Hope, Fortitude ; that we are commanded to do the same " Corporal Works," to feed, give drink, and clothe. Nay, that we have to fight the same things. There are four " Sins crying to Heaven for Vengeance " ; only four, but two of these are Murder and the Sin of Sodom, and the other two are Oppression of the poor and Defrauding the labourers of their wages. You will find, moreover, " Seven Deadly Sins " which you will see at once are just the anti-social sins which you are fighting—Pride, Covetousness, Lust, Anger, Gluttony, Envy, Sloth ; and you will observe that, with one exception, none of these seven shock the respectable public, though Socialism does. You will further observe that four of these sins—Pride, Covetousness, Envy, and Sloth, and often Gluttony as well—are popularly regarded as very gentleman-like qualities.

Will you, then, realize—and it is time you did !—that what you and every good man are fighting is nothing else than wickedness, and none the less wickedness because it is embodied in statute-books and economic formulæ ? Beneath all your political work you have to convert the heart of man. And it is a tough job. You won't convert him by pointing to his interests. He is singularly blind about them, and always has been. You will only convert him by giving him a moral ideal. Is there a better one than

Christ ?   If so, how is it that Socialism can only be spread
in those countries where the people have professed the
Christian faith for many hundreds of years ?   The Church
has made plenty of mistakes, and its members have com-
mitted ruinous sins like other people, and always there have
been many Judases within the camp selling the Christ for
pieces of silver ; but its united voice, its official documents,
its pattern saints have never faltered ; and at least it has
driven into men's hard hearts some touch of brotherly love,
and has made Socialism already almost possible in Christian
countries.

This Socialism is its own old teaching revived.   It is
getting to understand that ; and the age of social lethargy
and religious competition is passing away.   Every Socialist
who understands how deeply religion has been concerned
in every movement that has ever won the enthusiasm of
men, every Socialist who realizes how enormous is the work
before him, must welcome the assistance of this ancient
and imperishable organ of love and justice.   And every
Christian who rejoices in the singular growth of religious
zeal in recent years must long to see all that huge force
given to the service of the Humanity which Jesus Christ
has taken up into the Godhead.

For the man that loves much is a Socialist, and the man
that loves most is a saint, and every man that truly loves
the brotherhood is in a state of salvation.

We know that we have passed from death unto life,
Because we love the brethren.

IV. A WORD OF REMEMBRANCE AND CAUTION TO THE RICH

By JOHN WOOLMAN

INTRODUCTION

" People may have no intention to oppress, yet by entering on expensive ways of life their minds may be so entangled therein, and so engaged to support expensive customs, as to be estranged from the pure sympathizing spirit." (Remarks on Sundry Subjects. First printed, London, 1773.)

JOHN WOOLMAN, the author of this hundred-year-old tract, lived in the New England Colonies in the days when they still paid allegiance (and taxes) to the British Government.

He is usually known as a Quaker advocate of the cause of the slave at a time when slave-holding was still looked on, even by most of his co-religionists, as an essential part of the normal and heaven-ordained state of society. It is, however, frequently overlooked that he perceived clearly that the question of slavery was but one phase of the labour question. He wrote not only *Some Considerations on the Keeping of Negroes*, but also *On Merchandizing, On Trading in Superfluities, On Schools.* In his writings he enunciates, in simple religious phraseology, some of the truths which economists are only now beginning to understand ; he is, as it were, the voice in the wilderness, the John the Baptist of the gospel of Socialism.

The following essay contains the most connected account of his views on social questions. Though first printed in

1793, it was probably written about 1771, shortly before Woolman's death, and not long before the publication of *The Wealth of Nations*. But the ten years spent by Adam Smith at Glasgow University and Balliol College, Oxford, were passed by his American contemporary in work on his father's farm and in a small country store. So that the question naturally arises, by what authority is it that the working tailor says these things ? Woolman's answer may be found in his Journal : his writings are " openings from the Lord," his words are spoken " from an inward knowledge that they arise from the heavenly spring." " There is," says Woolman, writing in 1762 on the keeping of negroes, " a principle which is pure, placed in the human mind, which in different places and ages hath had different names ; it is, however, pure and proceeds from God. It is deep and inward, confined to no forms of religion nor excluded from any, when the heart stands in perfect sincerity. In whomsoever this takes root and grows, they become brethren."

John Woolman was, he tells us in his Journal, " born in Northampton, in Burlington County, West Jersey, in the year 1720." He was one of a large family, and, his parents being Quakers, he was brought up in conscientious Puritan fashion. He received " schooling pretty well for a planter," probably at the small country school of the village. This he supplemented by work in winter evenings, and with much reading of " the Holy Scriptures and religious books." Till he was about twenty-one he lived with his parents and worked on his father's farm. Then he left home for the neighbouring village of Mount Holly, New Jersey, " to tend shop and keep books " for " a man in much business as a shopkeeper and baker." Here, in a small Quaker community, he made his home, and the plain, two-storey, whitewashed house in which he lived was standing fifty years ago, still overlooking a country rich with farms and woodlands. Here, on the 18th of eighth month, 1749, he was married to " a well-inclined damsel," Sarah Ellis ; and here he brought up his little family.

But it was not his lot to die in this spot where he had

passed so much of his life. In 1772 he felt a "religious concern" "to visit Friends [Quakers] in the northern parts of England." Notwithstanding the wishes of his friends, he thought it right to travel "steerage," and doubtless suffered from the thirty-eight days' voyage across the Atlantic. In his journeying through England he usually went about on foot in order to avoid participating in the cruelties under which post-boys and stage-horses suffered. Five months after leaving home he fell a victim to smallpox, and died at York on the 7th of tenth month, 1772.

His business career illustrates the principles he advocated. Perceiving that "a humble man with the blessing of the Lord might live on a little," he learned the trade of tailoring and settled down in Mount Holly as a tailor, with a small retail business in trimmings, linings, and cloth—in spite of the temptation to enter the lucrative calling of general storekeeper, and his "natural inclination to merchandise." But even in his tailor's shop "trade increased every year, and the way to large business" in cloths and linen appeared open; but he tells us, "I felt a stop in my mind," "believing that Truth required me to live more free from outward cumbers." Not without some regret, some natural longing after the position of ease and wealth which he might have won for his family, he laid down merchandise in 1756 and lived as a working tailor without even an apprentice. Part of the time and energy thus freed from the cares of this world he devoted to tending his garden and orchard, believing that "if the leadings of the Spirit were more faithfully attended to" . . . "more people would be engaged in the sweet employment of husbandry, and in the path of pure wisdom, labour would be an agreeable healthful employment." He gained leisure, moreover, to write many valuable essays, and to undertake journeys through the States in the service of the slaves. It is probable that his work was an important factor in the ultimate abolition of slavery.

The whole life of Woolman was a protest against superfluities. He saw with singular clearness that "every degree of luxury hath some connection with evil." Thus it is to an excess of fatigue, to an "increase of labour beyond

that which our Heavenly Father intends," that he attri-
butes the undue use of spirituous liquors among the poor.
He held " that if such as had great estates generally lived
in that plainness and humility which belong to a Christian
life, and laid much easier rents and interests on their lands
and moneys, and thus led the way to a right use of things,
so great a number of people might be employed in things
useful, that labour both for men and other creatures would
need to be no more than an agreeable employ, and divers
branches of business, which serve chiefly to please the
natural inclinations of our minds, and which at present
seem necessary to circulate that wealth which some gather,
might, in this way of pure wisdom, be discontinued "—an
idea which he expanded in Section IV of this pamphlet.
He carried his principles into even the smallest details of
life.   He did not feel easy to drink from vessels of silver
at the house of a friend.   He stipulated in his last illness
that no medicines should be given that come " through
defiled channels or oppressive hands."   Believing that the
dyeing of garments injured the material and led to un-
cleanliness, he gradually adopted a costume of " natural
coloured " garments ; yet he suffered much from the fear
of ridicule, especially as light-coloured hats were coming
into fashion at the time, and his motives might therefore
be misunderstood !   There is wonderful pathos in his
simple account of these and other of his practices ; and
there is much practical sense in his longing that " people
might come into cleanness of spirit, cleanness of person,
and cleanness about their houses and garments."

The following extracts constitute about one-half of the
pamphlet.   Omissions are, in every case, indicated, and
the headings have been added by the editors.   The whole
may be found in an edition of *The Journal of John Woolman*,
with an Introduction by the poet Whittier, published by
Headley Bros., 14 Bishopsgate Street Without, E.C.

SECTION I

WEALTH desired for its own sake obstructs the increase of
virtue, and large possessions in the hands of selfish men
have a bad tendency, for by their means too small a num-

ber of people are employed in useful things, and some of
them are necessitated to labour too hard, while others
would want business to earn their bread, were not employments invented which, having no real usefulness, serve
only to please the vain mind.

RESULTS OF HIGH RENTS

Rents on lands are often so high that persons of but
small substance are straitened in taking farms, and while
tenants are healthy and prosperous in business, they often
find occasion to labour harder than was intended by our
gracious Creator. Oxen and horses are often seen at work
when, through heat and too much labour, their eyes and
the motions of their bodies manifest that they are oppressed. Their loads in wagons are frequently so heavy
that when weary with hauling them far, their drivers find
occasion in going up hills or through mire, to get them
forward by whipping. Many poor people are so thronged
in their business that it is difficult for them to provide
shelter for their cattle against the storms. These things
are common when in health, but through sickness and in-
ability to labour, through loss of cattle, and miscarriage in
business, many are so straitened that much of their increase goes to pay rent, and they have not wherewith to
buy what they require.

Hence one poor woman, in providing for her family and
attending the sick, does as much business as would for the
time be suitable employment for two or three ; and honest
persons are often straitened to give their children suitable
learning. The money which the wealthy receive from the
poor, who do more than a proper share of business in
raising it, is frequently paid to other poor people for doing
business which is foreign to the true use of things.

" UNIVERSAL LOVE " AS AGAINST LAWS AND CUSTOMS.

Men who have large estates and live in the spirit of
charity ; who carefully inspect the circumstances of those
who occupy their estates, and, regardless of the customs of
the times, regulate their demands agreeably to universal love,

being righteous on principle, do good to the poor without placing it to an act of bounty. Their example in avoiding superfluities tends to excite moderation in others; their uprightness in not exacting what the laws and customs would support them in tends to open the channel to moderate labour in useful affairs, and to discourage those branches of business which have not their foundation in true wisdom. . . .

God's Ownership

The Creator of the earth is the owner of it. He gave us being thereon, and our nature requires nourishment from the produce of it. He is kind and merciful to his creatures; and while they live answerably to the design of their creation, they are so far entitled to convenient subsistence that we may not justly deprive them of it.

Man's Tenure

By the agreements and contracts of our predecessors, and by our own doings, some enjoy a much greater share of this world than others; and while those possessions are faithfully improved for the good of the whole, it agrees with equity; but he who, with a view to self-exaltation, causeth some to labour immoderately, and with the profits arising therefrom employs others in the luxuries of life, acts contrary to the gracious designs of him who is the owner of the earth; nor can any possessions, either acquired or derived from ancestors, justify such conduct. Goodness remains to be goodness, and the direction of pure wisdom is obligatory on all reasonable creatures.

Though the poor occupy our estates by a bargain, to which they in their poor circumstances agree, and we may ask even less than a punctual fulfilling of their agreement, yet if our views are to lay up riches, or to live in conformity to customs which have not their foundation in the truth, and our demands are such as require from them greater toil or application to business than is consistent with pure love, we invade their rights as inhabitants of a world of which a good and gracious God is the proprietor, and under whom we are tenants.

Were all superfluities and the desire of outward greatness laid aside, and the right use of things universally attended to, such a number of people might be employed in things useful as that moderate labour with the blessing of Heaven would answer all good purposes, and a sufficient number would have time to attend to the proper affairs of civil society.

. . . . . .

SECTION IV

Our blessed Redeemer, in directing us how to conduct ourselves one towards another, appeals to our own feelings : " Whatsoever ye would that men should do to you, do ye even so to them."

How the Poor Live

Now, when some who have never experienced hard labour themselves live in fullness on the labour of others, there is often a danger of their not having a right feeling of the labourer's condition, and of being thereby disqualified to judge candidly in their case, not knowing what they themselves would desire, were they to labour hard from one year to another to raise the necessaries of life and pay high rent besides. It is good for those who live in fullness to cultivate tenderness of heart, and to improve every opportunity of being acquainted with the hardships and fatigues of those who labour for their living ; and thus to think seriously with themselves, Am I influenced by true charity in fixing all my demands ? Have I no desire to support myself in expensive customs, because my acquaintances live in such customs ?

The Golden Rule

If a wealthy man, on serious reflection, finds a witness in his own conscience that he indulges himself in some expensive customs which might be omitted consistently with the true design of living, and which, were he to change

places with those who occupy his estate, he would desire
to be discontinued by them ; whoever is thus awakened
will necessarily find the injunction binding : " Do ye even
so to them." Divine love imposeth no rigorous or un-
reasonable commands, but graciously points out the spirit
of brotherhood and the way to happiness, in attaining
which it is necessary that we relinquish all that is selfish.

SECTION V

" As Others See Us "

Let us reflect on the condition of a poor innocent man,
on whom the rich man, from a desire after wealth and
luxuries, lays heavy burdens ; when this labourer looks
over the cause of his heavy toil and considers that it is
laid on him to support that which hath no foundation in
pure wisdom, we may well suppose that an uneasiness
ariseth in his mind towards one who might without any
inconvenience deal more favourably with him. When he
considers that by his industry his fellow-creature is benefited and sees that this wealthy man is not satisfied with
being supported in a plain way, but to gratify a desire of
conforming to wrong customs increaseth to an extreme
the labours of those who occupy his estate, we may reason-
ably judge that he will think himself unkindly used.
When he considers that the proceedings of the wealthy
are agreeable to the customs of the times, and sees no
means of redress in this world, how will the sighings of this
innocent person ascend to the throne of that great and
good Being who created all, and who hath a constant care
over his creatures ! He who toils year after year to furnish
others with wealth and superfluities, until by overmuch
labour he is wearied and oppressed, understands the meaning of that language, " Ye know the heart of a stranger,
seeing ye were strangers in the land of Egypt."

Many at this day who know not the heart of a stranger
indulge themselves in ways of life which occasion more
labour than Infinite Goodness intends for man, and yet
compassionate the distresses of such as come directly

nder their observation; were these to change circum-
tances awhile with their labourers, were they to pass
egularly through the means of knowing the heart of a
stranger and come to a feeling knowledge of the straits and
ardships which many poor innocent people pass through
ι obscure life; were these who now fare sumptuously
very day to act the other part of the scene until seven
mes had passed over them and return again to their
ormer states,

The Golden Rule Once More.

believe many of them would embrace a less expensive
fe, and would lighten the heavy burdens of some who
ow labour out of their sight, and who pass through straits
ith which they are but little acquainted. To see their
llow-creatures under difficulties to which they are in no
egree accessory tends to awaken tenderness in the minds
: all reasonable people; but if we consider the condition
: those who are depressed in answering our demands, who
bour for us out of our sight while we pass our time in
llness, and consider also that much less than we demand
ould supply us with things really useful, what heart will
ot relent, or what reasonable man can refrain from miti-
ating that grief of which he himself is the cause, when he
ay do so without inconvenience?

.   .   .   .   .   .

SECTION VII

Accumulation of Wealth for our Children

If by our wealth we make our children great, without a
ll persuasion that we could not bestow it better, and
ius give them power to deal hardly with others more
rtuous than they, it can after death give us no more
tisfaction than if by this treasure we had raised others
oove our own, and had given them power to oppress
iem. . . .

Christ's Teaching

The greater part of the necessaries of life are so far

perishable that each generation hath occasion to labour
for them ; and when we look towards a succeeding age
with a mind influenced by universal love, instead of en-
deavouring to exempt some from those cares which necessarily relate to this life, and to give them power to oppress
others, we desire that they may all be the Lord's children
and live in that humility and order becoming his family.
Our hearts, being thus opened and enlarged, will feel
content with a state of things as foreign to luxury and
grandeur as that which our Redeemer laid down as a
pattern. . . .

For, as he lived in perfect plainness and simplicity, the
greatest in his family cannot by virtue of his station claim
a right to live in worldly grandeur without contradicting
him who said, " It is enough for the disciple to be as his
Master." . . .

The Tyranny of Selfishness

Tyranny as applied to a man riseth up and soon has an
end ; but if we consider the numerous oppressions in many
states, and the calamities occasioned by contending nations
in various countries and ages of the world, and remember
that selfishness hath been the original cause of them all ;
if we consider that those who are unredeemed from this
selfish spirit not only afflict others but are afflicted them
selves, and have no real quietness in this life nor in futurity
but, according to the sayings of Christ, have their portion
" where the worm dieth not and the fire is not quenched "
if we consider the havoc that is made in this age, and how
numbers of people are hurried on, striving to collect trea
sure to please that mind which wanders from perfect
resignedness, and in that wisdom which is foolishness with
God are perverting the true use of things, labouring as in
the fire, contending with one another even unto blood, and
exerting their power to support ways of living foreign to
the life of one wholly crucified to the world ; if we con
sider what great numbers of people are employed
preparing implements of war, and the labour and toil of
armies set apart for protecting their respective territori

from invasion, and the extensive miseries which attend their engagements ; while they who till the land and are employed in other useful things in supporting not only themselves but those employed in military affairs, and also those who own the soil, have great hardships to encounter through too much labour ; while others in several kingdoms are busied in fetching men to help to labour from distant parts of the world, to spend the remainder of their lives in the uncomfortable condition of slaves, and that self is the bottom of these proceedings ;—

THE EXAMPLE OF CHRIST

amidst all this confusion, and these scenes of sorrow and distress, can we remember that we are the disciples of the Prince of Peace, and the example of humility and plainness which he set for us, without feeling an earnest desire to be disentangled from everything connected with selfish customs in food, in raiment, in houses, and in all things else ? That being of Christ's family, and walking as he walked, we may stand in that uprightness wherein man was first made, and have no fellowship with those inventions which men in their fallen wisdom have sought out.

SECTION IX

. The way of carrying on wars common in the world is so far distinguishable from the purity of Christ's religion that many scruple to join in them. Those who are so redeemed from the love of the world as to possess nothing in a selfish spirit have their " life hid with Christ in God," and he preserves them in resignedness, even in times of commotion.

As they possess nothing but what pertains to his family, anxious thoughts about wealth or dominion have little or nothing in them on which to work ; and they learn contentment in being disposed of according to his will who, being omnipotent and always mindful of his children, causeth all things to work for their good ; but when that spirit works which loves riches, and in its working gathers

F

wealth and cleaves to customs which have their root in self-pleasing, whatever name it hath it still desires to defend the treasures thus gotten.

CONNECTION BETWEEN WEALTH AND WAR

This is like a chain in which the end of one link encloseth the end of another. The rising up of a desire to obtain wealth is the beginning ; this desire being cherished, moves to action ; and riches thus gotten please self ; and while self has a life in them it desires to have them defended Wealth is attended with power, by which bargains and proceedings contrary to universal righteousness are sup ported ; and hence oppression carried on with worldly policy and order, clothes itself with the name of justice and becomes like a seed of discord in the soul. And as a spirit which wanders from the pure habitation prevails, so the seeds of war swell and sprout and grow and become strong until much fruit is ripened. Then cometh the harvest spoken of by the prophet, which " is a heap in the day of grief and desperate sorrows." Oh, that we who declare against wars, and acknowledge our trust to be in God only may walk in the light, and therein examine our foundation and motives in holding great estates ! May we look upon our treasures, the furniture of our houses and our gar ments, and try whether the seeds of war have nourishment in these our possessions. Holding treasures in the self pleasing spirit is a strong plant, the fruit whereof ripen fast. A day of outward distress is coming, and Divine love calls to prepare against it.

SECTION X

THE EARTH ONLY A CONDITIONAL GIFT

" The heaven, even the heavens, are the Lord's ; but the earth hath he given to the children of men." As se vants of God our land or estates we hold under him as h gifts ; and in applying the profits it is our duty to a consistently with the designs of our Benefactor. Imperfe men may give from motives of misguided affection, b perfect wisdom and goodness gives agreeably to his own nature; nor is this gift absolute, but conditional, for us to occupy as dutiful children and not otherwise; for he alone is the true proprietor. "The world," saith he, "is mine, and the fulness thereof."

The inspired lawgiver directed that such of the Israelites as sold their inheritance should sell it for a term only, and that they or their children should again enjoy it in the year of jubilee, settled on every fiftieth year. "The land shall not be sold forever, for the land is mine, saith the Lord, for ye are strangers and sojourners with me." This was designed to prevent the rich from oppressing the poor by too much engrossing the land; and our blessed Redeemer said : "Till heaven and earth pass, one jot or one tittle shall in no wise pass from the law, till all be fulfilled."

When Divine love takes place in the hearts of any people, and they steadily act in a principle of universal righteousness, then the true intent of the law is fulfilled, though their outward modes of proceeding may be various; but when men are possessed by that spirit hinted at by the prophet, and, looking over their wealth, say in their hearts, "Have we not taken to us horns by our own strength?" they deviate from the Divine law, and do not count their possessions so strictly God's nor the weak and poor entitled to so much of the increase thereof, but that they may indulge their desires in conforming to worldly pomp.

THE LUST FOR LAND

Thus when house is joined to house and field laid to field, until there is no place, and the poor are thereby straitened, though this is done by bargain and purchase, yet so far as it stands distinguished from universal love, so far that woe predicted by the prophet will accompany their proceedings. As he who first founded the earth was then the true proprietor of it, so he still remains, and though he hath given it to the children of men, so that multitudes of people have had their sustenance from it while they continued here, yet he hath never alienated it, but his right is as good as at first; nor can any apply the increase of their possessions contrary to universal love, nor dispose of lands in a way which they know tends to exalt some by oppressing others without being justly chargeable with usurpation.

SECTION XII

While our minds are prepossessed in favour of customs distinguishable from perfect purity, we are in danger of not attending with singleness to that light which opens to our view the nature of universal righteousness.

THE DIVISION OF LABOUR

In the affairs of a thickly-settled country are variety of useful employments besides tilling the earth ; so that for some men to have more land than is necessary to build upon and to answer the occasions of their families may consist with brotherhood ; and from the various gifts which God hath bestowed on those employed in husbandry, for some to possess and occupy much more than others may likewise so consist ; but when any, on the strength of their possessions, demand such rent or interest as necessitates their tenants to a closer application to business than our merciful Father designed for us, it puts the wheels of perfect brotherhood out of order, and leads to employments the promoting of which belongs not to the family of Christ, whose example in all points being a pattern of wisdom, the plainness and simplicity of his outward appearance may well make us ashamed to adorn our bodies with costly array or treasure up wealth by the least oppression.

RIGHT AND ' RIGHTS "

Though by claims grounded on prior possession great inequality appears among men ; yet the instructions of the Great Proprietor of the earth are necessary to be attended to in all our proceedings as possessors or claimers of the soil. " The steps of a good man are ordered of the Lord," and those who are thus guided and whose hearts are enlarged in his love give directions concerning their possessions agreeably thereto ; and that claim which stands on universal righteousness is a good right ; but the continuance of that right depends on properly applying the profits thereof. The word " right " commonly relates to our possessions. We say, a right of propriety to such a division of a province, or a clear, indisputable right to the land within certain bounds. Thus this word is continued as a remembrancer of the original intent of dividing the land by boundaries, and implies that it was equitably or rightly divided, that is, divided according to righteousness. In this—that is, in equity and righteousness—consists the strength of our claim. If we trace an unrighteous claim and find gifts or grants proved by sufficient seals and witnesses it gives not the claimant a right ; for that which is opposite to righteousness is wrong ; and the nature of it must be changed before it can be right.

AN UTOPIA

Suppose twenty free men, professed followers of Christ, discovered an island, and that they with their wives, independent of all others, took possession of it and, dividing t equally, made improvements and multiplied; suppose these first possessors, being generally influenced by true love, did with paternal regard look over the increasing condition of the inhabitants, and, near the end of their lives, gave such directions concerning their respective possessions as best suited the convenience of the whole and tended to preserve love and harmony ; and that their successors in the continued increase of people generally followed their pious example and pursued means the most effectual to keep oppression out of their island ; but that one of these first settlers, from a fond attachment to one of his numerous sons, no more deserving than the rest, gives the chief of his lands to him, and by an instrument sufficiently witnessed strongly expressed his mind and will ;—

TWENTIETH PART OF UTOPIA UNDER A LANDLORD

Suppose this son, being landlord to his brethren and

nephews, demands such a portion of the fruits of the earth
as may supply himself, his family and some others, and
that these others thus supplied out of his store are employed in adorning his building with curious engravings
and paintings, preparing carriages to ride in, vessels for his
house, delicious meats, fine wrought apparel and furniture,
all suiting that distinction lately arisen between him and
the other inhabitants ; and that, having the absolute dis-
posal of these numerous improvements, his power so increaseth that in all conferences relative to the public
affairs of the island, these plain, honest men, who are
zealous for equitable establishments, find great difficulty
in proceeding agreeably to their righteous inclinations—
suppose this son, from a fondness to one of his children,
joined with a desire to continue this grandeur under his
own name, confirms the chief of his possessions to him, and
thus for many ages there is one great landlord over near a
twentieth part of this island, and the rest are poor oppressed
people, to some of whom, from the manner of their education, joined with a notion of the greatness of their predecessors, labour is disagreeable ; who, therefore, by artful
applications to the weakness, unguardedness, and corrup-
tions of others in striving to get a living out of them,
increase the difficulties among them, while the inhabitants
of other parts, who guard against oppression and with one
consent train up their children in frugality and useful
labour, live more harmoniously ;—

" Quo Warranto ? "

If we trace the claims of the ninth or tenth of these great
landlords down to the first possessor and find the claim
supported throughout by instruments strongly drawn and
witnessed, after all we could not admit a belief into our
hearts that he had a right to so great a portion of land
after such a numerous increase of inhabitants.

The first possessor of that twentieth part held no more,
we suppose, than an equitable portion ; but when the Lord,
who first gave these twenty men possession of this island
unknown to all others, gave being to numerous people who

inhabited the twentieth part, whose natures required the fruits thereof for their sustenance, this great claimer of the soil could not have a right to the whole to dispose of it in gratifying his irregular desires ; but they, as creatures of the Most High God, Possessor of heaven and earth, had a right to part of what this great claimer held, though they had no instruments to confirm their right.

CONCLUSION

Thus oppression in the extreme appears terrible ; but oppression in more refined appearances remains to be oppression, and when the smallest degree of it is cherished it grows stronger and more extensive.

To labor for a perfect redemption from this spirit of oppression is the great business of the whole family of Christ Jesus in this world.

THE END

PUBLICATIONS OF THE FABIAN SOCIETY.

FABIAN BOOKS.

Fabian Essays in Socialism. Edited by Bernard Shaw. 40,000 sold. Paper 1s., cloth 2s., post-free.

This Misery of Boots. By H. G. Wells. Fcap. 8vo. Paper 3d., post-free 4d., or 2s. 3d. per dozen, post-free 2s. 7d.

Fabianism and the Empire. Edited by Bernard Shaw. Post-free 1s. 1½d.

Fabian Tracts. Bound. Complete set of those in print. 1 vol. Buckram 4s. 6d., post-free 5s.

FABIAN TRACTS.

1d. each (postage ½d.), or 9d. per dozen (postage 3d.), unless stated otherwise.

I. *On Socialism in its Various Aspects.*

No.
51. **Socialism True and False.** By Sidney Webb, L.C.C.
5. **Facts for Socialists.** 10th Edition. Revised 1906.
7. **Capital and Land.** 6th Edition. Revised 1904.
45. **The Impossibilities of Anarchism.** By Bernard Shaw. 2d.
69. **The Difficulties of Individualism.** By Sidney Webb.
113. **Communism.** By William Morris.
107. **Socialism for Millionaires.** By Bernard Shaw.
15. **English Progress towards Social Democracy.** By Sidney Webb.
72. **The Moral Aspects of Socialism.** By Sidney Ball, M.A.
133. **Socialism and Christianity.** By Rev. Percy Dearmer.
42. **Christian Socialism.** By Rev. Stewart D. Headlam.
78. **Socialism and the Teaching of Christ.** By Rev. John Clifford.
87. **A Welsh Translation of No. 78.**

II. *On the Application of Socialism to Particular Problems.*

Municipal and State Control of Industry.

No.
128. **The Case for a Legal Minimum Wage.**
125. **Municipalization by Provinces.**
119. **Public Control of Electric Power and Transit.**
123. **The Revival of Agriculture. A National Policy.**
115. **State Aid to Agriculture.** By T. S. Dymond.
121. **Public Service versus Private Expenditure.** By Sir Oliver Lodge.
84. **The Economics of Direct Employment.**
122. **Municipal Milk and Public Health.** By Lawson Dodd.
86. **Municipal Drink Traffic.** 4th Edition, 1905.
85. **Liquor Licensing at Home and Abroad.** [P.T.O.

No.   *Housing.*

76. **Houses for the People.** A description of the powers of local authorities for housing.

103. **Overcrowding in London and its Remedy.** By W. C. Steadman, M.P.

109. **Cottage Plans and Common Sense.** By Raymond Unwin.

No.   *Factory Acts and Conditions of Labour.*

112. **Life in the Laundry.** A summary of conditions and reforms.

130. **Home-work and Sweating.** By Miss B. L. Hutchins.

48. **Eight Hours by Law.** A practical solution.

23. **The Case for an Eight Hours Bill.**

47. **The Unemployed.** By John Burns, M.P.

88. **State Arbitration and the Living Wage.** 2nd ed.

75. **Labor in the Longest Reign.** By Sidney Webb.

No.   *Other Problems.*

136. **The Village and the Landlord.** By Edward Carpenter.

135. **Paupers and Old Age Pensions.** By Sidney Webb.

131. **The Decline in the Birth Rate.** By Sidney Webb.

126. **The Abolition of Poor Law Guardians.**

120. **"After Bread, Education."**

118. **Secret of Rural Depopulation.** By D. C. Pedder.

111. **Reform of Reformatories and Industrial Schools.**

98. **State Railways for Ireland.**

124. **State Control of Trusts.** By H. W. Macrosty, B.A.

14. **The New Reform Bill.** A draft scheme.

82. **The Workman's Compensation Act, 1906.**

III. *On General Politics and the Policy of Fabian Society.*

No.

127. **Socialism and Labour Policy.**

116. **Fabianism and the Fiscal Question.** An alternative policy.

108. **Twentieth Century Policy.** By Sidney Webb.

70. **Report on Fabian Policy** (to Internat. Socialist Workers).

41. **The Early History of the Fabian Society.** By Bernard Shaw.

40. **The Fabian Election Manifesto, 1892.**

IV. *On Books.*

No.

182. **A Guide to Books for Socialists.**

29. **What to Read.** A classified list. 4th edition. 6d. net.

129. **More Books to Read.** 1901–6.

A complete list of Tracts and Leaflets sent on application to the Secretary,

THE FABIAN SOCIETY, 3 CLEMENT'S INN, LONDON, W.C.

JUST PUBLISHED.

16 pages, size 14 × 9½ ; 7d. nett, Post free in tube 8d.

JESUS IN LONDON

By E. NESBIT.

**With six full-page and one half-page illustrations by
Spencer Pryse. In two colours.**

"A fine piece of work in every respect."—*Morning Leader.*

"A moving poem, full of strong, stirring passages."—
Christian World.

"A terrible indictment. Would it could hang in every
dining room."—*Young Man.*

"Very simple, pathetic and appealing is the poem-cry
which Mrs. Bland has written, and Mr. Spencer Pryse so
effectually pictured."—*Daily Chronicle.*

"Mr. Pryse has caught exactly the spirit of the verses.
If we may select one for mention we should choose the last,
an extraordinary picture of the Crucifixion."—*Daily News.*

"A touching and effective poem. Mr. Pryse is a young
artist of tremendous power and truth, and his 'low-life'
pictures are destined to become famous. We venture to
prophesy that those who buy this publication to-day will
have a commercially valuable possession ten years hence."
—*The Clarion.*

LONDON: A. C. FIFIELD, 44 FLEET STREET, E.C.

A searching and illuminating study of the conditions of rural labour in England to-day, revealing their disastrous effects on the morals, physique, and persistence of the agricultural labourer.

WHERE MEN DECAY

A SURVEY OF PRESENT RURAL CONDITIONS.

By LIEUT.-COL. D. C. PEDDER.

Crown 8vo.   Cloth gilt.   2s. 6d. nett.   Postage 3d.

Mr. C. F. G. Masterman, M.P., writing in *The Daily News* of January 1, 1908, of this book, under the heading of "A Book of the Day" (1¼ columns), says:—"Living in the heart of the country, passionately on the side of the poor, and revolting against the apathy and stupidity which is bringing that country into decay, he (Col. Pedder) writes from the inspiration of an ardent advocate of reform. He writes well: with insight, with humour, with eloquence. No one could accept this as an impartial picture of English village life, or refuse to recognize that there is another side. But no one could deny that the great central fact of these present discontents is unchallengeable. Here is the Rural Exodus, the 'Rural Depopulation,' interpreted in terms of flesh and blood. . . . This is a book which will exasperate, sometimes excite protest, sometimes acceptance. But it is a living book, written from the heart of a man. A book to read."

"A welcome and timely picture. . . . An instructive and luminous work."—*Leicester Post.*

"This is a book to make you almost despair of the future of your country."—A. E. Fletcher, in *The Clarion.*

LONDON: *A. C. FIFIELD,* 44 *FLEET STREET,* E.C

TOLSTOY : A STUDY

By PERCY REDFERN.

With Photo.

Crown 8vo wrappers 1s. *nett, post free* 1s. 1½d.; *cloth gilt* 2s. 3d.

" An excellent and excellently written critical study."
—*Mr. H. G. Wells.*

" It is simply and ably written. It is both very interesting and very full of information."—*Evening News.*

" It ought to be of real value to Englishmen who want to understand Tolstoy."—*Mr. Aylmer Maude* (*Tolstoy's translator*).

" It is obvious that Mr. Redfern has a right to be heard."—*Sheffield Independent.*

" As a sane at the same time sympathetic review of a great man and a great work this book may confidently be recommended."—*Daily News.*

" We do not think anything in Tolstoy in so small a compass surpasses this book. It is well informed, sane, and balanced . . . All concerned in the social movements of our times would find profit in perusing it."—*Methodist Times.*

THE REASONABLE LIFE

By ARNOLD BENNETT.

6d. *nett, postage* 1d.; *quarter cloth gilt top,* 1s. *nett.*

" Mr. Bennett is one of the very few writers of our day who have the power of simultaneously delighting the man in the street and the critic in the study."—*Liverpool Post.*

LONDON : A. C. FIFIELD, 44, FLEET STREET, E.C.

THE TRUTH ABOUT THE LORDS

FIFTY YEARS OF OUR NEW NOBILITY, 1857–1907.

By JOSEPH CLAYTON,

Author of " The Bishops as Legislators," " Bishop Westcott," etc.

Crown 8vo, wrappers, 1s. nett, post free 1s. 1½d. ; cloth gilt, post free, 2s. 3d.

" Uncommonly useful."—*The Tribune.*

" Establishes an irresistible impeachment of the hereditary law-makers."—*Leicester Post.*

." Mr. Clayton has done excellent service in telling the truth about our hereditary legislators. The degradation of the House of Lords is too shocking for words."—*The Clarion.*

" Mr. Clayton's volume will prove indispensable to the modern political reformer. As a caustic commentary on the anti-Lords Campaign, and an arsenal of facts, it is without an equal."—*New Age.*

BY THE SAME AUTHOR.

THE BISHOPS AS LEGISLATORS

Third Edition. Wrappers 1s. nett, postage 1½d ; cloth 2s. 3d.

" This is a tremendous and terrible indictment, which can only be supported by an appeal to facts. Unfortunately for the bishops, the record is black. It could not be much worse."—*Daily News.*

LONDON : A. C. FIFIELD, 44, FLEET STREET, E.C.

THE FABIAN SOCIALIST SERIES

consists of a revised, collected, and classified edition of some of the most valuable of the famous "Fabian Tracts" in a style more suitable for the general reading public, and supplying in a handy and attractive form the best and most authoritative thought on "What Socialism Means." Each booklet contains not less than 96 well-printed pages, good paper and good type, and is supplied in two forms, i.e., in attractive wrappers at 6d. each, nett, and in quarter cloth boards, gilt top, at 1/- each, nett. *Postage 1d. and 2d. each respectively.*

VOLUMES NOW READY:

LONDON: A. C. FIFIELD, 44 FLEET STREET, E.C.

43

293

71 131   A C   55 1

131